THE COMPASSIONATE LEADERSHIP MODEL AND PYRAMID

Ascending Empathy: Unveiling the Seven-level Journey of Compassionate Leadership

The Journey of a **Compassionate Leader**

From i to "We"

Serving Others

Society: Model citizenship

Community: Corporate responsibilty, etc.

Organization: People investors, customers and employees

Local environment: Neighbors well-being, local business

Next of kin: Family, Spouse, children, siblings, significant others and friends

Self-compassion: Good health, education self-development, and positive attitude

The Compassionate Leadership Pyramid   (khoureis, 2021)

DR. ABRAHAM KHOUREIS, Ph.D.

Copyright Notice

THE COMPASSIONATE LEADERSHIP MODEL AND PYRAMID

Ascending Empathy: Unveiling the Seven-level Journey of Compassionate Leadership

The Journey of a
Compassionate
Leader

From i to "We"

Serving Others

Society: Model citizenship

Community: Corporate responsibilty, etc.

Organization: People investors, customers and employees

Local environment: Neighbors well-being, local business

Next of kin: Family, Spouse, children, siblings, significant others and friends

Self-compassion: Good health, education self-development, and positive attitude

The Compassionate Leadership Pyramid   (khoureis, 2021)

DR. ABRAHAM KHOUREIS, PH.D.

This page intentionally left blank for your reading reflection

_____

_____

_____

_____

_____

_____

_____

_____

_____

_____

ENDORSEMENTS AND PRAISES

for

"The Compassionate Leadership Model and Pyramid"

"Leaders are born when they replace 'I' with 'We.' This is a journey of self-discovery and compassion. Compassionate leaders serve others selflessly, without expecting anything in return. In his powerful book, *The Compassionate Leadership Model and Pyramid*, the Global Guru of Compassionate Leadership Dr. Abraham Khoureis shares a roadmap that guides people and leaders to be more caring and understanding and thus secure the success of their teams."
Oleg Konovalov, The da Vinci of Visionary Leadership, Author of *The Vision Code*

"Dr. Abe's book explores not only the value of compassionate leadership through the levels of the pyramid, but how to make it happen. His ideas about being considerate to others, listening to understand, caring with real intent, and collaborating to grow together are exceptional ideas to demonstrate compassionate leadership." **Dr. Dave Ulrich, Rensis Likert Professor, Ross School of Business, University of Michigan – Father of our Modern HR**

"A manager takes care of 'things.' A leader tells people 'what to do.' As Dr. Abraham Khoureis so eloquently describes, the future of leadership is a multifaceted journey that encompasses self-awareness, mindfulness, empathy, and a genuine commitment to the well-being of those being led. Brilliant read for anyone who is or wishes to be a leader in the 21st century." **Amb. Terry Earthwind Nichols, 10-Time Internationally Published Author, Speaker, and 'Top 10 Thought Leader'**

"The world certainly needs more compassion, now more than ever, and it absolutely has to happen with our leaders. Abe is absolutely at the right place, at the right time, and with a model and approach that makes it easier for all of us to think, act, and lead with more compassion..." **Dr. Len Jessup, President of Claremont Graduate University**

Dr. Abraham Khoureis has developed a compelling model for individuals and organizations to develop the practice of compassionate leadership. Khoureis builds on his Compassionate Leadership Pyramid, which starts with individual introspection and self-awareness and gradually moves outwards towards consideration of and authentic commitment to the well-being of increasingly broader levels of relationships. Drawing on extensive research,

Dr. Khoureis uncovers the impacts of leadership practices on motivating people to think beyond their own needs and serve others. Supported by research data and practical examples, Khoureis's new book does indeed make a case for compassionate leadership and how organizations can implement it effectively. **Dr. Karen Linkletter, Research Director at MLARI, author**

"What sets Dr. Abe Khoureis' Compassionate Leadership Pyramid Model apart is not just its innovative approach, but its timeliness. In an era marred by divisiveness and strife, this model serves as a much-needed reminder of our shared humanity. Its foundation of self-awareness and empathy encourages leaders to prioritize understanding their own emotions while encouraging genuine connections with others. By emphasizing active listening, collaboration, and inspirational leadership, Dr. Khoureis provides a transformative framework that not only enhances organizational success but also promotes a culture of compassion and understanding in today's challenging environment." **Ken Pasternak, Author, Educator, Consultant, Speaker**

"Dr. Abe has done it again! His work as a global thought leader in business and education continues, releasing a powerful new book about a leadership trait that is all too rare—compassion. While you may find a great deal written about empathy, it's rare that you'll see much about compassion. Compassion picks up where empathy leaves off. *The Compassionate Leadership Model and Pyramid* helps readers stand on the shoulders of their personal growth and become compassionate leaders to their core. If you're looking for what's next in leadership, this book is for you." **Leo Bottary, Founder & Managing Partner of Peernovation, LLC; Adjunct Professor, Rutgers University**

"Dr. Abraham Khoureis cares deeply about compassionate leadership, as demonstrated in *The Compassionate Leadership Model and Pyramid.* His important book provides current and aspiring leaders with a concrete vision they can build upon now and in the future." - **Bruce Rosenstein, Managing Editor, *Leader to Leader*, author of *Create Your Future the Peter Drucker Way***

"Dr Abraham Khoureis' new book - The Compassionate Leadership Model and Pyramid - is a wonderfully enlightening work. It provides a logically powerful and effective tool to guide leaders and other interested people on a truly transformative and empowering journey. Organizations need to balance the 4Rs of growth for sustainable success – Revenue, Risk, Reputation as underpinned by Relationships. This new book provides a light to achieve this through dealing with essential issues such as sell-awareness, emotional intelligence and mindfulness. I highly recommend this book." **Simon Haigh – Author – Business Growth Expert**

"Dr. Khoureis' case for the Compassionate Leader is compelling because it embodies trust, caring, and serving characteristics that transcend all people, cultures, and geographies. It may be the essential competency for successful leadership in today's complex world where people are yearning to contribute their time, energy, and talents to places worthy of their commitment." **Michele Hunt, Transformation Catalyst, Author of** *DreamMakers: Innovating for the Greater Good*

"To have a lasting impact - which is what all of us hope to have, you cannot simply call for compassion. Nor can you only declare your intension to be compassionate and consider the job completed. To truly have impact that longed for rippling impact to others and to the world, you have to 'understand' compassion, model it, know how to seed it in others. In short, you must embody compassion in all you do. That is the goal and the gift of

Dr. Abraham Khoureis's Compassionate Leadership Model and Pyramid - a uniquely robust guide to cultivating this most powerful of ways of being. Show yourself a little compassion and begin your journey today with this helpful hopeful guide." **Larry Robertson, Internationally-acclaimed, award-winning author of Rebel Leadership: How to Thrive in Uncertain Times**

In Dr. Abraham Khoureis' latest book, "Compassionate Leadership Model and Pyramid," he explains the seven levels of compassionate leadership based on research that supports the value of creating a compassionate culture. What impacted me most was his point about practicing an intention being different from practicing an action. We know we must be curious, empathetic, good listeners, and communicate well. But how do we do that? That is where Dr. Khoureis' work excels by guiding us on how to reach our goals.

We know compassion ties into improved outcomes at work, but if you don't know where you are right now regarding these seven levels, how can you improve yourself? His compassionate leadership pyramid serves as a roadmap that can make you more self-aware and empathetic and teach you how to foster a corporate culture by emulating what you have learned. It is a must-read for leaders who know what they want as an outcome but don't know how to get there! **Dr. Diane Hamilton, Ph.D., Nationally Syndicated Radio Show Host, Speaker, Author, Thinkers50 Radar.**

"Dr. Abe Khoureis's new book, "The Compassionate Leadership Model and Pyramid" gives us the seven steps to achieving this level of Compassionate Leadership. Today, more than ever, we need leaders who can help their teams achieve success through empathetic management - a methodology that will help us build sustainable businesses in the long term. Dr. Khoureis's Model will be a "must read" for anyone who wants to build a better future for our working world. A very needed manuscript for this day and age!" **Lauren Ackerman, Entrepreneur and Philanthropist.**

"Dr. Abraham Khoureis is the father of compassionate leadership. I enjoyed reading "The Compassionate Leadership Model and Pyramid." Compassion is key to leadership in today's world. It is a great book. It is a must-read." **Professor M.S. Rao, Ph.D.—The Father of "Soft Leadership" & International Leadership Guru.**

This page intentionally left blank for your reading reflection

_____

_____

_____

_____

_____

_____

_____

_____

_____

_____

_____

Table of Contents

Foreword 1

Preface 5

Acknowledgments 9

Introduction..13

Chapter 1: What Is Compassion and 19
Where Does It Come From? 19

Chapter 2: Characteristics of Compassionate Leaders 25

Chapter 3: The Compassionate Leadership Pyramid..........33

Chapter 4: Self-Compassion – Level 1 35

Chapter 5: Next of Kin – Level 2 43

Chapter 6: Local Environment – Level 3.....................53

Chapter 7: Organization – Level 4 63

Chapter 8: Community – Level 5.................................73

Chapter 9: Society – Level 6......................................85

Chapter 10: Serving Others – Level 7 95
The Compassionate Noble Leader................................95

Chapter 11: Comparison of Leadership Models..............85

Chapter 12: Turning Data into Insights 117

Chapter 13: Consequences and Benefits 127
of Compassionate Leadership....................................127

Chapter 14: The Journey of Compassionate Leadership....139

Chapter 15: Glossary..147

References 155

This page intentionally left blank for your reading reflection

_____

_____

_____

_____

_____

_____

_____

_____

_____

_____

_____

Foreword

for the

The Compassionate Leadership Model and Pyramid

By

Dr. Dave Ulrich, Rensis Likert Professor, Ross School of Business, University of Michigan

I remember as a child throwing a rock in a pond and seeing the ripples that emerged from the splash.

I did not fully appreciate the profound impact of this simple ripple effect (sometimes called butterfly, domino, or snowball effect) where a single action has expanded complex consequences. A plant opening or closing has layers of impact on a community. Monetary policy decisions may impact consumer decisions. Thought leaders and Influencers shape opinions and actions of many.

The compassionate leader model and pyramid by Dr. Abraham Khoureis exemplifies this ripple effect for leadership. When leaders have self-compassion, their ripple effect moves up the Compassionate Leadership Pyramid to increasingly broad social networks, ultimately creating a more compassionate society.

Employees often observe and do what their leaders do. Actions often speak louder than words. Francis of Assisi, a 13th century monk, is attributed as saying, "Preach the gospel at all times and if necessary, use words." Leaders lead by example. When leaders show compassion for themselves and for those in their immediate network, others will not only experience compassion, but likely want to pass it along to others.

I have learned this compassion within my family when I treat my spouse and children with kindness, grace, and charity, they likely respond in kind. In my professional work, I have learned that turning my harshness into benevolence helps me build positive relationships that foster growth. The logic of the golden rule of doing for others what you would have them to unto you fosters a virtuous cycle of affirmation.

Dr. Abe's book explores not only the value of compassionate leadership through the levels of the pyramid, but how to make it happen. His ideas about being considerate to others, listening to understand, caring with real intent, and collaborating to grow together are exceptional ideas to demonstrate compassionate leadership.

In our world today, where bickering, snipes, barbs, and insults are de rigueur, contempt dismantles respect, enmity disables empathy, and helplessness replaces hope. If each of us could recognize, apply, and demonstrate the compassion that Dr. Abe proposes, we would see the ripple effect where caring, charity, and sympathy prevail.

We would like to live in this world, and it is possible if we start with ourselves and those closest to us.

This page intentionally left blank for your reading reflection

_____

_____

_____

_____

_____

_____

_____

_____

_____

_____

_____

Preface

As I began to write this book, I found myself contemplating a simple yet profound question: What is at the heart of truly effective leadership? The answer, as I discovered, is not found in assertiveness, strategic cunning, or even visionary thinking, but rather in a quality that is far more human and universally accessible: **compassion**.

"The Compassionate Leadership Model and Pyramid," is an exploration and a guide. It is born out of years of observation, experience, research, and a deep-seated belief in the transformative power of compassionate leadership. It seeks to challenge traditional notions of leadership that prioritize dominance and control, advocating instead for a leadership style rooted in understanding, empathy, and a genuine concern for others.

The journey through the pages of this book is structured around a seven-level pyramid, a framework model that I have developed through careful study, research, and reflection. This pyramid is not just a metaphor but a practical model, guiding readers from the foundational level of self-compassion to the pinnacle of becoming a compassionate leader who serves others without receiving anything in return, a leader who inspire and enact positive change on a societal level.

Each chapter presented here is thoughtfully crafted to explore a distinct level of the Compassionate Leadership Model and Pyramid, beginning with self-compassion in Level 1 and culminating in the ultimate realization of a compassionate noble leader in Level 7. The journey is intentionally designed to be sequential, with each level building upon the foundation of the previous ones, reflecting the progressive and interconnected nature of developing true compassionate leadership. Additional chapters delve into the core characteristics of a compassionate leader and provide actionable recommendations for aspiring compassionate leaders.

To further enrich the reader's experience, as a bonus, the book references section has online links to a curated selection of articles authored by me and previously published in national magazines and websites, offering practical insights and real-world applications of the principles discussed.

In writing this leadership journey, I have from my professional experiences and from a diverse range of fields including psychology, neuroscience, philosophy, and spiritual teachings. This interdisciplinary approach has enriched the content, providing a well-rounded perspective on how compassionate leadership can be nurtured and manifested in various aspects of life.

This book is intended for anyone who is leading or aspires to be a leader, regardless of their current role or position. It is my hope that it will serve as both a guide and an inspiration, encouraging readers to embark on their own journey towards compassionate leadership. By doing so, we can not only transform our own lives but also make a significant, positive impact on the world around us. Welcome to a journey of discovery, challenges, growth, and transformation. Welcome to a path less traveled, but immensely challenging and rewarding. Welcome to the journey of compassionate leadership.

This page intentionally left blank for your reading reflection

---

Acknowledgments

Writing The Compassionate Leadership Model and Pyramid has been an enlightening journey, not only of intellect but also of soul and spirit. This book is the result of a deep and personal exploration into what it means to lead with compassion. I am grateful to all who have inspired me throughout the years.

First and foremost, I am profoundly grateful to my Creator who gifted me with an enlightened mind and a kind compassionate heart. To my family, and loved ones, your unwavering love, patience, and encouragement have been the foundation upon which this work stands. To my colleagues, mentors, and peers in the professional realm, I extend my heartfelt appreciation.

Your constructive feedback, shared wisdom, and diverse perspectives have been invaluable in shaping this work. A special thanks to my esteemed colleagues and friends, Dr. Dave Ulrich, for your unwavering support and for being a beacon of wisdom when I needed it most, and Dr. Edwin Locke, for your insightful guidance and advice on how to effectively formulate this model toward a theory. Your expertise and generosity have been instrumental in bringing this vision to life.

I am also deeply grateful to my colleagues and friends who have so graciously endorsed and praised the work presented in this book. Your encouragement and validation mean more to me than words can express. Thank you all for your contributions, which have enriched this journey and strengthened the foundation of this awesome work.

This book is also a tribute to the academic and research community whose dedication to advancing our understanding of leadership and compassion has shaped the foundation of my ideas. I am indebted to the scholars and thought leaders whose work has illuminated this path and whose insights have contributed to the framework of this book.

To the team at the book publisher, book distributor, bookstore chains, individual stores, and libraries: thank you for believing in the importance of this message and for your dedication to ensuring it reaches readers. To each of you who has contributed to making this work a reality: your participation in this research, contributions, attention to detail, and thoughtful suggestions have been invaluable in refining this final model. For that, I am deeply grateful. I owe a great deal of gratitude to the countless leaders whose lives and legacies have inspired this book. Their journeys serve as powerful reminders of the profound impact compassionate leadership can have on individuals, organizations, and society.

To the communities and groups, I have been fortunate to engage with, thank you for your encouragement and the thought-provoking conversations that have shaped my understanding of leadership in diverse contexts. Your insights have made this book richer and more grounded. To my students, thank you!

Lastly, to you, the readers, thank you for your willingness to explore the profound and transformative journey of compassionate leadership. Your commitment to this path is a source of hope for a better, more empathetic future.

This book is as much yours as it is mine. It is the result of shared learning, shared wisdom, and a collective aspiration to make leadership synonymous with compassion. Thank you for being part of this journey.

Introduction

In an era where leadership often seems to be synonymous with power, influence, and dominance, "The Compassionate Leadership Model and Pyramid" emerges as a transformative guide, proposing a radically different approach. This book is not just a treatise on leadership; it is a journey, of "ascend and descend" a seven-level pyramid that redefines what it means to lead with compassion. Each level on this pyramid represents a crucial stage in the development of a leader who is not just effective, but profoundly impactful in the most humanly positive way.

Compassionate leadership is essential in today's world because it bridges the divide created by complexity, uncertainty, and polarization. Amid rapid technological advances, global crises, and social upheavals, people are searching for leaders who not only understand their struggles but actively work to ease them. Compassionate leadership creates environments of trust, inclusion, and collaboration, allowing individuals to thrive while addressing the collective challenges of our time. By prioritizing empathy, compassion, and shared humanity over rigid authority, such leaders inspire others to rise above personal gain, encouraging a culture where innovative solutions emerge through mutual support and respect. In this divided humanity, compassionate leadership offers clarity and purpose, guiding communities toward resilience and unity

At the heart of this book is a simple yet profound truth: compassionate leadership is not a fixed trait, but a journey of growth and understanding that starts from within and radiates outward, touching every aspect of our lives. The seven levels of the pyramid provide a structured pathway for this journey, starting from the core of self-compassion and extending to the noblest form of leadership that influences society at large.

Level 1: Self-Compassion is where it all begins. It involves understanding and improving oneself, embracing personal strengths and weaknesses, and developing a gentle and supportive inner dialogue. This foundation is crucial because a leader who cannot show compassion toward themselves will find it challenging to authentically extend that compassion to others. At its core, self-compassion is about striving to become better, not just for our own growth, but to better serve and uplift those around us.

Level 2: Next of Kin – Our Own Tribe delves into the realm of close relationships: family, friends, and those we consider our inner circle. It explores how compassionate leadership begins at home and in our personal interactions, shaping the way we connect with those closest to us. This is our base that will eventually help lift us as we initially help lift them up.

Level 3: Local Environment takes the concept of compassion beyond the personal sphere, applying it to the local communities in which we live. It examines how leaders can create a sense of belonging, understanding, and mutual support in their immediate social environments.

Level 4: Organization shifts the focus to the professional sphere. Here, I discuss how workplaces and learning institutions thrive when guided by compassionate leadership, developing environments where creativity, innovation, and collaboration flourish. Employees feel valued and productive, shareholders benefit from ethical, sustainable practices, and leaders inspire teams through mutual respect and purpose. Consumers, in turn, gain trust and loyalty through improved products and services. Compassionate leadership is the cornerstone of progress and resilience in this interconnected ecosystem.

Level 5: Community broadens the scope further, encapsulating the wider community in which we participate. This is where the impact of compassion begins to ripple outwards, influencing larger groups and creating a culture of empathy and support.

Level 6: Society represents the penultimate level of the pyramid. This level tackles the broader societal impact of compassionate leadership, showing how leaders can effect positive change on a grand scale, influencing policies, social norms, and cultural values.

Level 7: Serving Others - The Compassionate Noble Leader who serves others without receiving anything in return is the culmination of this journey. It portrays the ideal of a leader who has mastered all levels of the pyramid. This leader is not just a figure of authority but a beacon of hope, integrity, and profound human empathy, inspiring and uplifting everyone they touch.

"The Compassionate Leadership Model and Pyramid" is more than a book; it's a manifesto for a new era of leadership. It invites you, the reader, to embark on this journey, challenging you to travel through the journey of the pyramid and embrace a form of leadership that can transform organizations, lives, and societies.

This page intentionally left blank for your reading reflection

Chapter 1

What Is Compassion and
Where Does It Come From?

We may ask, why are some leaders compassionate while others are not? To answer this question, we must address the question of what compassion is and where it comes from.

Compassion is an intricate and vital element of human nature, arising from a blend of biological, psychological, environmental, and cultural factors. Its origins can be explored through the lenses of human evolution, individual experiences, and conscious personal development. It also originates from a deep understanding of our shared humanity and the intrinsic value of serving others.

For this exploration and leadership model, compassion is defined as the act of caring for and supporting those around us without expecting anything in return. At its core, compassion is rooted in empathy, the ability to connect with others on an emotional level, and a genuine desire to alleviate suffering or contribute to their well-being. It is not merely a fleeting feeling but a conscious choice to prioritize kindness, understanding, and action in our interactions.

True compassion transcends transactional relationships. It embodies the principle of giving without seeking personal gain, a commitment to uplifting others simply because it is the right thing to do. In organizational contexts, this means creating environments where decisions and practices reflect a dedication to the greater good, ensuring that employees, customers, and communities feel valued and supported. Compassion is the foundation upon which trust, collaboration, and meaningful change are built, serving as a guiding force for leaders who aspire to make a lasting impact.

In my research for this model, I found that compassion is deeply rooted in our biology, likely emerged as a survival mechanism essential for mending social bonds and cooperative behaviors that strengthened early communities. Neuroscience underscores this biological foundation, with empathetic responses activating specific regions of the brain, such as the anterior insula and anterior cingulate cortex. These findings highlight how compassion is not merely a social construct but an integral part of human physiology.

On a psychological level, individual traits and emotional well-being shape one's capacity for compassion. People with heightened emotional awareness, spiritual, or natural empathy are often more compassionate. However, mental health challenges can either enhance or inhibit this ability, depending on how they influence emotional connection with others. Early childhood experiences further play a pivotal role in shaping compassion. Caregivers who model compassion set the foundation for a child's ability to empathize, while life experiences, especially those involving adversity or exposure to diverse perspectives, deepen this trait over time.

Social and cultural contexts also significantly influence the expression and cultivation of compassion. Cultural norms and societal expectations shape how compassion is perceived and practiced, with schools and communities either cultivating or stifling its growth. Meanwhile, philosophical and spiritual traditions elevate compassion as a core virtue. Teachings from religious and spiritual texts, for example, view compassion as a religious duty or a pathway to spiritual enlightenment, encouraging individuals to integrate it into their daily lives. Importantly and interestingly, I discovered that compassion is not solely an innate trait, it can be deliberately developed. Practices like mindfulness, meditation, religious supplications, and self-reflection allow individuals to enhance their ability for empathy and connection. This deliberate cultivation transforms compassion into a conscious and impactful way of engaging with the world, enriching personal growth and strengthening the fabric of society.

Understanding the Development of the Compassionate Leader

Developing into a compassionate leader requires a deep understanding of the organizational environment and a commitment to personal growth and self- development. While there is ongoing debate about whether great leaders are born or made, I firmly believe that leadership is shaped by the environment in which one works and lives. Even individuals with innate leadership qualities must actively develop and cultivate these research-based characteristics and traits over time to become effective compassionate leaders.

In my understanding, "compassion" goes beyond mere sympathy or pity. Compassionate leaders genuinely strive to understand and share the feelings of their followers and act on it. To develop empathy and compassion, it is essential to genuinely attempt to comprehend others' perspectives and emotions. This can be achieved by putting oneself in their shoes, truly immersing oneself in their experiences, and acting on it using that understanding to make informed decisions that genuinely benefit the individuals involved.

Whereas practicing empathy is the intention, while practicing compassion is the action.

EMPATHY = INTENTION
COMPASSION = ACTION

Intention + Action = Empathetic Compassion

Intention − Action =
Missed opportunity to serve others.

Formula of Practicing Compassion   (Khoureis, 2021–2025)

Leaders are always eager to learn and grow. They read, attend workshops, and seek mentors to get better at what they do. This helps them stay updated and become better leaders.

Chapter 2

Characteristics
of Compassionate Leaders

Compassionate leadership is defined by a set of characteristics that distinguish leaders who prioritize empathy, understanding, and the well-being of others. These leaders strive to create environments where individuals feel valued, respected, and empowered to reach their full potential. By embodying these traits, compassionate leaders not only enhance their organizations but also inspire trust, collaboration, and meaningful change. Below are the key characteristics that define a compassionate leader:

Adaptability: Compassionate leaders are adaptable. It gives them the ability to adjust and respond effectively to changing circumstances, challenges, and the unique needs of individuals or teams. It reflects a leader's flexibility and open-mindedness, enabling them to maintain empathy and compassion while navigating dynamic environments and making decisions that align with their values and the well-being of others.

Caring: Caring is at the core of compassionate leadership. Leaders must genuinely show care and kindness to their followers, complementing their consideration of them. Demonstrating acts of kindness and empathy can encourage a sense of trust and support within the team.

Concern for Well-being: Concern for the well-being of followers is another crucial characteristic of compassionate leaders. Making their followers' well-being a priority, leaders show kindhearted concern and actively work to help them improve, achieve, and grow. It is essential for leaders to communicate that their concern is genuine and meant to support the development and success of their followers.

Empowering Others: Compassionate leaders create a supportive work environment that prioritizes the well-being and growth of their team members. They prioritize work-life balance and employee well-being by supporting flexible work arrangements and implementing initiatives that promote physical and mental health. A supportive work environment nurtures compassionate leaders and empowers individuals to thrive.

Flexibility: Compassionate leaders see flexibility as the capacity to embrace change and modify their approaches to suit evolving circumstances and diverse needs. It highlights their willingness to adapt their mindset and strategies while maintaining empathy and a focus on the well-being of others.

Active Listeners: Compassionate leaders seek to know how others feel and what they think. They pay close attention when people talk, showing real interest in what they are saying. This makes people trust and connect with them because they feel like their thoughts and feelings matter.

Lead by Example: Compassionate leaders are mindful of the importance of their roles in their environment. Intentionally, they become a role model for compassionate leadership. They demonstrate kindness, fairness, and respect in their interactions with others. They treat all individuals with dignity and encourage an inclusive environment where everyone feels valued and respected. They show appreciation for the contributions of their team members and celebrate their successes. Leading by example sets the tone for compassionate behavior and creates a positive ripple effect throughout the organization.

Mindful: Compassionate leaders practice mindfulness, remaining fully present and engaged in the moment. They cultivate an awareness of their thoughts, emotions, and actions, ensuring they align with their values and intentions. By practicing mindfulness, they enhance their ability to respond with empathy and understanding to the needs of others, encouraging deeper connections and creating an environment of care and trust.

Open Communicator: Leaders who care about their team's well-being make sure that feedback is welcome and important. They often ask their team for their thoughts and really listen to what they have to say. They encourage open and truthful conversations, making sure everyone feels okay sharing their ideas, worries, and suggestions. When they engage in this kind of honest two-way communication, it helps them build trust, strengthen relationships, and create an atmosphere where people can work together, develop, and come up with new ideas.

Practice Serving Others: The compassionate leader's primary focus is on serving others. Adopting a mindset of service and a genuine desire to help others succeed, they take the time to understand the needs and aspirations of their team members and provide the necessary support and resources to help them achieve their goals. By putting the needs of others first, they cultivate a culture of compassion, trust, and collaboration.

Recognize and Celebrate Compassionate Actions:
Compassionate leaders acknowledge and celebrate acts of compassion within their organization. They recognize individuals who demonstrate compassionate leadership and highlight their positive impact on others. By shining a light on compassionate behaviors, they reinforce the importance of compassion and inspire others to follow suit. Celebrating compassion creates a culture that values and encourages compassionate actions throughout the organization.

Resiliency: Compassionate leaders see resiliency as the ability to endure and recover from challenges or setbacks while keeping a steady focus on empathy and support for others. It reflects their strength in navigating adversity, adapting to difficulties, and creating a positive, encouraging environment that inspires confidence and perseverance in those they lead.

Self-Reflection and Self-Awareness: It begins by engaging in self-reflection and developing into self-awareness. Leaders take the time to assess their strengths and weaknesses, identify areas for personal growth, and gain a deeper understanding of their values and purpose. They engage in practices such as mindfulness, meditation, religious prayers, chants, or supplication to enhance self-awareness and develop a deeper connection with their thoughts, spiritual selves, emotions, and behaviors.

The Ability to Collaborate: A key skill, compassionate leaders can effectively work with others while leading their followers, both within the organization and beyond. Internal collaboration involves working across functional and organizational boundaries, building teamwork and cooperation. External collaboration extends to competitors and other organizations for the betterment of society. Open communication, setting clear organizational goals, and delegating authority and tasks as needed are critical components of the characteristics of compassionate leaders.

Thoughtful Consideration: Consideration of others is an important aspect of compassionate leadership. Leaders exercise thoughtful behavior and avoid causing unnecessary discomfort or harm to their followers. By setting the standard of mutual respect and creating a working environment where such respect is practiced, leaders can earn the loyalty and trust of their followers. Utilizing their influence and authority, compassionate leaders should strive to improve working conditions and encourage a positive and supportive atmosphere.

Understanding: Understanding is a vital quality that compassionate leaders have. They compassionately perceive the behaviors of their followers, recognizing that conflicts can serve as opportunities for growth and innovation. Tolerance, awareness of followers' feelings, and forgiveness for their shortcomings are essential. When conflicts arise, leaders should actively seek open feedback and explanations to gain a comprehensive understanding of the situation and to resolve any misunderstandings.

This page intentionally left blank for your reading reflection

_____

_____

_____

_____

_____

_____

_____

_____

_____

_____

_____

Chapter 3

The Compassionate Leadership Pyramid

The Compassionate Leadership Pyramid is a powerful framework that helps leaders grow and apply compassion in every part of their lives and work.

This visual model combines ideas from other leadership approaches into one clear and practical structure. Each level guides leaders to first develop compassion within themselves and then extend it to their families, communities, organizations, and beyond. It provides a clear roadmap for leaders to create meaningful connections, inspire positive change, and grow into noble and compassionate leaders who make a difference in the world.

Level 1: Self-Compassion
Level 2: Next of Kin – Our Own Tribe
Level 3: Local Environment
Level 4: Organization

Level 5: Community

Level 6: Society

Level 7: Serving Others - The Compassionate Noble Leader

The Journey of a **Compassionate Leader**

From i to "We"

- Serving Others
- **Society:** Model citizenship
- **Community:** Corporate responsibilty, etc.
- **Organization:** People investors, customers and employees
- **Local environment:** Neighbors well-being, local business
- **Next of kin:** Family, Spouse, children, siblings, significant others and friends
- **Self-compassion:** Good health, education self-development, and positive attitude

The Compassionate Leadership Pyramid   (khoureis, 2021)

Chapter 4

Self-Compassion – Level 1
The Foundation of Compassionate Leadership

In the journey of compassionate leadership, self-compassion emerges as an essential cornerstone. It is not merely an act of self-kindness but a deliberate, transformative process that empowers leaders to serve others effectively. By nurturing themselves holistically, in education, health, wealth, and emotional well-being, leaders establish a foundation for meaningful and sustainable societal change. This foundation is not solely for individual growth but is essential for cultivating the growth and stability of those closest to them, their immediate family and community, who form the base of their broader impact.

Self-compassion begins with understanding its true nature: it is the act of caring for oneself without indulgence, balanced by the intention to become better equipped to support others. It involves prioritizing personal growth and well-being, not out of selfishness, but as a prerequisite for effective leadership. Leaders who invest in their own development become sources of strength, resilience, and inspiration for their teams and communities. By aligning self-compassion with purpose, leaders set a standard for holistic well-being that resonates across their spheres of influence.

Education is a pivotal catalyst for this transformation. It serves as the foundation of personal and societal growth. By expanding their intellectual horizons, leaders cultivate the empathy and wisdom needed to address the complexities of the world. This intellectual growth not only benefits the leader but also enables them to guide others with insight and understanding. Education equips leaders with the tools to tackle systemic challenges, innovate solutions, and promote inclusivity in their organizations and communities.

Compassionate leaders view **education** as a lifelong pursuit. It goes beyond formal schooling to include continuous learning, curiosity, and self-reflection. By staying informed and open to innovative ideas, leaders enhance their ability to connect with diverse perspectives and drive meaningful change. This commitment to learning becomes a ripple effect, inspiring those around them to pursue knowledge and growth.

Physical and mental well-being are integral to the journey of self-compassion. Leaders who prioritize their health ensure they have the energy, clarity, and resilience needed to navigate challenges and support others. Physical health involves maintaining regular exercise, balanced nutrition, and sufficient rest, creating a strong foundation for sustained leadership. Mental health, equally critical, requires practices like mindfulness, stress management, and seeking support when needed.

Compassionate leaders understand that neglecting health can lead to burnout, decreased productivity, and strained relationships. By valuing their well-being, they model the importance of self-care to their teams and communities. This emphasis on health cultivates an environment where well-being is prioritized, creating a culture of balance and resilience.

Wealth, when approached with intention and empathy, becomes a powerful tool for societal upliftment. Leaders who cultivate financial stability and prosperity can use their resources to create opportunities for others. This does not mean hoarding wealth for personal gain but leveraging it to invest in initiatives that benefit the greater good. For instance, funding educational programs, supporting small businesses, or contributing to community projects are ways leaders can use wealth to drive positive change.

Compassionate leaders view wealth to amplify their impact. They understand that financial security enables them to focus on higher purposes, such as mentoring others, supporting innovation, or addressing social inequities. By aligning their financial goals with their values, leaders demonstrate that prosperity and purpose can coexist, reinforcing the principles of compassionate leadership.

At the core of self-compassion is emotional well-being. It is the foundation of a leader's ability to empathize, connect, and inspire. Emotional well-being involves cultivating inner peace, practicing forgiveness, and embracing self-love. Leaders who invest in their emotional health are better equipped to navigate conflicts, manage stress, and develop positive relationships. Mindfulness practices, such as meditation or journaling, enhance emotional resilience by helping leaders stay present and grounded. This presence enables leaders to respond thoughtfully rather than react impulsively, creating an atmosphere of trust and understanding. Emotional well-being also enhances leaders' capacity to inspire and motivate others, demonstrating the power of compassion in action.

These interconnected elements, education, health, wealth, and emotional wellbeing, form the foundation of self-compassion. They are not isolated practices but parts of a holistic journey that prepares leaders to lead with purpose. Investing in oneself is a continuous process that benefits not only the individual but also their immediate family and broader community.

When leaders nurture their own growth, they create a ripple effect that empowers those around them to thrive. Families and close-knit communities serve as the first circle of influence for compassionate leaders. By modeling self-compassion, leaders inspire their loved ones to prioritize their well-being and development. This foundation of mutual support strengthens familial bonds, creating a resilient network that extends to the wider community. For example, when parents invest in their own growth, they set an example for their children, instilling values of education, health, and emotional balance that ripple outward.

The impact of self-compassion extends far beyond the individual. It begins within the family, where actions and attitudes set the tone for future generations. Leaders who prioritize self-compassion inspire their family members to do the same, creating a culture of support, growth, and resilience.

This foundation serves as a springboard for broader societal impact, where communities benefit from the collective well-being of their members. As self-compassionate leaders extend their influence, they inspire collective growth and resilience within their communities. The values they embody, empathy, understanding, and service, become catalysts for positive change. By encouraging others to embark on their journeys of self-improvement, leaders create a ripple effect that transforms individuals, families, and societies.

Self-compassion is not a destination; it is an ongoing process of growth and renewal. It requires leaders to continuously evaluate and nurture their education, health, wealth, and emotional well-being. This commitment to self-care is not an act of selfishness but a recognition of the interconnectedness between personal growth and collective well-being. By investing in themselves, leaders become better equipped to address challenges, inspire change, and serve others. The journey of self-compassion demands intentionality and perseverance. It requires leaders to confront their vulnerabilities, embrace their imperfections, and cultivate a mindset of continuous learning and improvement. By doing so, they set an example for others, demonstrating that self-compassion is the foundation of transformative leadership.

A Call to Action

The path to self-compassion is a call to action for leaders at every level. It is an invitation to invest in oneself as a means of serving others. Begin by asking: How can I nurture my own growth to better support those around me? What steps can I take to enhance my education, prioritize my health, manage my resources, and cultivate emotional resilience?

Start today with small, intentional actions. Commit to lifelong learning, adopt selfcare practices, and align your financial goals with your values. Embrace mindfulness as a tool for emotional well-being and prioritize meaningful connections with those closest to you. Remember, self-compassion is not a luxury; it is a responsibility that empowers you to lead with purpose and create a lasting impact.

When leaders prioritize self-compassion, they not only transform themselves but also inspire change in their families, communities, and organizations. By filling their own cup, they create a ripple effect of positivity and support that extends far beyond their immediate circle. Together, we can build a world where compassion begins within and radiates outward, shaping a brighter future for all.

Chapter 5

Next of Kin – Level 2
Uplifting Family Members and Our Own Tribe

After setting up the foundation of self-compassion, the natural progression leads us to the next level of compassionate leadership, focusing on our next of kin, family, significant others, children, siblings, and what we call here our "own tribe." By "own tribe," we refer to a personalized support system, the people we actively build around us as we grow on this journey. While the vision of a unified society is admirable, where individuals belong to their country and humanity at large, nurturing our own tribe is a critical step. This intimate focus not only fortifies personal relationships but also prepares us to integrate into and contribute effectively to the broader society, enabling change and unity on a larger scale.

Our family and our own tribe function as the anchors of our lives, providing essential support, love, and encouragement. These bonds are not one-sided; they thrive on mutual effort, open communication, and compassion. By investing time and energy into these connections, we not only strengthen our immediate circle but also create ripples of positivity that extend into the broader community. Understanding and valuing each member of this circle is crucial. Everyone brings their own unique strengths, perspectives, and challenges, contributing to the rich tapestry of relationships that define our lives.

Every relationship within our family and tribe requires a tailored approach. Whether it involves a spouse, child, sibling, or parent, each bond demands unique care and attention. Spouses and significant others, for example, often serve as mirrors, reflecting our strengths and vulnerabilities. Compassionate leadership within a partnership involves open communication, mutual respect, and a shared commitment to growth. Effective partnerships thrive on understanding and effort, creating a safe space for both individuals to flourish. Children, too, hold a special place in this dynamic. Their intuitive nature means they learn not just from what we say but from what we do.

Modeling self-compassion and empathy in our behavior allows them to internalize these values and carry them forward. By setting examples through actions, leaders within families inspire the next generation to prioritize kindness and understanding in their interactions with the world.

Siblings and extended family members play a vital role in our lives. These lifelong relationships carry a shared history that can serve as a source of strength or present challenges. Navigating these dynamics with empathy and a focus on shared values helps maintain strong ties. Even amidst disagreements, the commitment to understanding and mutual respect can strengthen these bonds over time, enriching the lives of all involved.

Our chosen tribe, friends and close confidants, is equally important. These are the people we actively choose to surround ourselves with, and their influence on our growth cannot be underestimated. A supportive tribe offers a sense of belonging and encouragement, becoming a source of resilience and inspiration. As the saying goes, we are the average of the five people we spend the most time with. Surrounding ourselves with compassionate, driven, and empathetic individuals motivates us to strive for personal and collective improvement.

Actively contributing to this tribe involves mutual investment. Compassionate leadership in these relationships means offering support, celebrating successes, and being present during challenging times. By cultivating trust and understanding, we create a community that uplifts each member and strengthens the collective bond. The impact of investing in our family and tribe extends far beyond immediate relationships.

When we nurture these bonds, we lay the groundwork for a supportive network that influences the broader community. Parents who model compassion and empathy for their children raise individuals who carry these values into the world. Similarly, strong partnerships inspire others to cultivate meaningful connections in their own lives.

This ripple effect shows the interconnectedness of compassionate leadership. Acts of kindness and understanding within our closest circles radiate outward, creating a culture of empathy and collaboration. Leaders who prioritize these values create environments where individuals feel valued and supported, enabling collective growth and resilience.

Building and supporting these relationships is not without its challenges. Conflicts and misunderstandings are inevitable, but they also present opportunities for growth and deeper connection. Approaching these moments with compassion and a willingness to listen transforms them into valuable lessons. Whether it involves addressing longstanding disagreements or navigating new dynamics, the commitment to understanding and empathy strengthens bonds over time.

Relationships with siblings often reflect both the shared joys and complexities of family life. These bonds, though sometimes strained by differences, carry the potential for deep connection and mutual support. By focusing on common ground and shared values, siblings can develop enduring relationships that enrich their lives and contribute to a sense of familial unity.

Each member of our family and tribe plays a unique role in this interconnected system. Parents provide guidance and support, nurturing the development of their children. Spouses and partners offer companionship and collaboration, creating a foundation of mutual respect and shared goals. Children inspire joy and hope, motivating their elders to invest in the future. Friends and chosen tribe members contribute diverse perspectives and encouragement, broadening our understanding of the world.

Compassionate leadership within these relationships involves recognizing and valuing these roles while offering support tailored to everyone. For parents, this might mean actively listening to their children and encouraging their dreams. For siblings, it could involve celebrating each other's achievements and providing a steady source of support. For friends, it means being present in both triumphs and challenges, offering a shoulder to lean on and a voice of encouragement.

Intentionality is key to cultivating strong and compassionate relationships. Setting aside dedicated time for loved ones, practicing active listening, and expressing gratitude are simple yet powerful ways to strengthen these bonds. By prioritizing these actions, leaders within families and tribes show their commitment to the well-being of their circle. Small gestures, such as reaching out to a sibling after an extended period of silence or expressing appreciation for a partner's support, can have a profound impact. These acts of kindness reinforce connections and create an atmosphere of trust and mutual respect. Over time, these efforts build a resilient network that serves as a foundation for broader societal contributions.

The journey of compassionate leadership through our next of kin, family, and own tribe is deeply rewarding. It allows us to create a network of support that not only enriches our own lives but also empowers us to make a greater impact on the world. As we invest in these relationships, we build a foundation of love and understanding that extends far beyond our immediate circle. These bonds are the building blocks of a compassionate society. By prioritizing our next of kin, family, and our own tribe, we not only enrich our own lives but also create a ripple effect that inspires others to do the same.

A Call to Action

Take the time to nurture your relationships with those closest to you. Reach out to a sibling you have not spoken to in a while. Schedule quality time with your spouse or significant other. Be present for your children, not just physically but emotionally. Show appreciation for your parents and the sacrifices they have made. Invest in your friends and own tribe, offering support and encouragement whenever possible.

Remember, every act of compassion strengthens the bonds that hold us together. These relationships are the building blocks of a compassionate society, and their impact extends far beyond our immediate circle. By prioritizing our next of kin, family, and our own tribe, we not only enrich our own lives but also create a ripple effect that inspires others to do the same. The journey of compassionate leadership is a collective one, and it begins with those closest to us.

Take the first step today. Reach out, connect, and invest in your family and own tribe. Together, we can create a world that is grounded in love, empathy, and understanding, one relationship at a time.

This page intentionally left blank for your reading reflection

———————————————————————

———————————————————————

———————————————————————

———————————————————————

———————————————————————

———————————————————————

———————————————————————

———————————————————————

———————————————————————

———————————————————————

———————————————————————

Chapter 6

Local Environment – Level 3
The Heart of Community Compassion

A thriving local environment is the cornerstone of a compassionate community. It is within our neighborhoods and towns that we first connect with others outside our immediate circles, forming the foundation of collective progress and shared responsibility. The local environment represents more than a geographical space; it is a network of relationships, businesses, schools, and healthcare systems that define the fabric of a community. Cultivating compassion in the local environment is not just an ideal but a necessary step toward broader societal change.

Building a compassionate local environment begins with immersion in the community. To understand the unique needs and challenges of neighbors, local businesses, schools, and healthcare facilities, active participation and genuine engagement are essential. Attending town hall meetings, volunteering for community projects, and participating in local events are more than civic duties; they are opportunities to listen, learn, and build meaningful connections. These interactions lay the groundwork for creating a network of mutual support and empathy that strengthens the bonds within the community.

Local businesses are vital to the strength and vitality of any community. These small enterprises provide jobs, encourage innovation, and add a unique character to neighborhoods. Supporting local businesses is not merely a financial act but a demonstration of solidarity and mutual care. Business owners often face significant challenges, from economic pressures to limited resources. By choosing to shop locally and building relationships with business owners and employees, community members contribute not just to economic growth but to a shared sense of connection and responsibility. This approach reinforces the idea that thriving local businesses are an integral part of a compassionate community.

Education and healthcare are equally essential pillars of a thriving local environment. Schools and healthcare facilities are more than institutions; they are lifelines that ensure the growth and well-being of community members. Volunteering time and resources to support educational programs, extracurricular activities, and mentorship initiatives empowers young minds and nurtures the leaders of tomorrow. Similarly, contributing to local healthcare efforts, whether through organizing health awareness campaigns, supporting overburdened clinics, or advocating for accessible care, help create a robust framework for community health. Investing in these pillars ensures that the entire community has the opportunity to flourish.

Community events play a pivotal role in nurturing unity and creating a shared sense of purpose. Festivals, cleanup drives, charity fundraisers, and neighborhood gatherings serve as platforms for dialogue, collaboration, and celebration. These events provide opportunities for individuals to voice their ideas, share their concerns, and work together to create solutions. For instance, neighborhood health fairs that bring together clinics, fitness experts, and wellness practitioners can offer free consultations and workshops, improving access to essential services while highlighting the collective strength of the community. Such events underscore the power of collaborative efforts to build compassionate connections.

A compassionate local environment prioritizes the well-being of vulnerable populations, including the elderly, those experiencing homelessness, individuals facing economic hardship, and marginalized groups. Programs designed to support these populations, such as meal deliveries, social activities, and access to resources, not only alleviate immediate challenges but also create a stronger sense of connection within the community. Simple acts, such as visiting elderly residents or providing meals to those in need, demonstrate the tangible impact of compassion and reinforce the value of empathy in everyday interactions.

The ripple effect of compassionate leadership within the local environment is profound. When individuals lead by example, their actions inspire others to contribute. Increased volunteerism, stronger support for local businesses, and a more empathetic approach to addressing community challenges are just a few of the positive outcomes. These changes cultivate a culture of shared responsibility and collaboration, where each member feels empowered to play a role in the community's success.

Strengthening educational and healthcare systems within the local environment also creates long-term benefits. Schools and clinics that receive consistent community support often experience improved outcomes, such as higher student achievement and better access to healthcare services. This support extends beyond financial contributions to include active engagement and advocacy. For instance, mentoring students, organizing educational workshops, or taking part in health awareness campaigns are all ways to contribute to the vitality of these institutions. When communities prioritize these efforts, they not only enhance individual lives but also build a stronger collective future.

Compassionate leadership in the local environment goes beyond addressing immediate needs; it involves creating a culture of empathy, collaboration, and shared progress. Transforming neighborhoods into networks of mutual support lays the foundation for broader societal change. As community members work together to improve their surroundings, they build a collective resilience that helps everyone. This approach also cultivates a sense of pride and ownership within the community, encouraging individuals to still be engaged and committed to their wellbeing.

Volunteering is a cornerstone of building compassionate local environments. By dedicating time and skills to community projects, individuals contribute to collective progress while forming meaningful connections. Whether it is helping to organize a neighborhood cleanup drive, tutoring students, or assisting in local food banks, every act of service strengthens the fabric of the community. Volunteering not only addresses immediate needs but also inspires others to take similar actions, creating a cycle of compassion and collaboration.

Another critical aspect of cultivating a compassionate local environment is addressing systemic barriers that hinder equity and access. Advocacy for inclusive policies, fair resource allocation, and community-driven initiatives plays a significant role in creating a supportive local framework. Leaders and residents must work together to find and address these challenges, ensuring that all members of the community have the opportunity to thrive. By championing equity and justice, local environments become models of compassionate leadership that inspire broader societal change.

Active engagement with local businesses also promotes sustainable development. By choosing to support environmentally conscious enterprises or encouraging local businesses to adopt sustainable practices, community members contribute to a healthier environment and a more resilient local economy. These efforts demonstrate that compassion for the planet is an integral part of building compassionate communities. Supporting businesses that prioritize sustainability ensures that local environments are still vibrant and viable for future generations.

Art and culture are powerful tools for encouraging compassion within local environments. Public art installations, cultural festivals, and community performances provide opportunities for individuals to connect, share their stories, and celebrate their shared humanity. These initiatives enrich the cultural fabric of neighborhoods and create spaces for dialogue and understanding. Encouraging local artists and cultural events not only highlight the diversity within communities but also strengthens their social bonds.

Addressing the well-being of vulnerable populations requires intentional programs and initiatives that emphasize dignity and empowerment. Community meal programs, job training initiatives, and accessible housing solutions are examples of practical approaches to supporting those in need. By creating pathways for individuals to achieve stability and self-sufficiency, these efforts reinforce the value of compassion and collaboration. When communities prioritize the needs of their most vulnerable members, they create an environment of inclusivity and mutual care.

Reflecting on the importance of cultivating compassion in the local environment reveals a simple truth: meaningful change begins at the grassroots level. By investing in our neighborhoods and towns, we create a ripple effect that extends to the larger society. Actions such as patronizing local businesses, volunteering time and skills, supporting schools and clinics, and taking part in community events are tangible ways to contribute. These efforts not only strengthen individual connections but also create a culture of empathy and collaboration that drives collective progress.

A Call to Action

The call to action is clear. Each one of us has the ability to make a meaningful difference in our local environment. Whether through small acts of kindness or larger community-driven projects, our efforts lay the foundation for a compassionate society. By focusing on our immediate surroundings, we can build a world where every neighborhood thrives, one compassionate action at a time. Take the first step today, connect with your community, engage in meaningful initiatives, and inspire others to join you in creating a brighter future for all.

This page intentionally left blank for your reading reflection

Chapter 7

Organization – Level 4
Crafting a Compassionate Enterprise

The role of a compassionate leader within an organization extends far beyond ensuring profitability. It encompasses the responsibility to add value to every aspect of the enterprise, addressing the needs of investors, leadership, employees, customers, and consumers alike. A compassionate organization operates with purpose, efficiency, and integrity, prioritizing ethical practices, holistic well-being, and meaningful contributions to society. At its core, such an organization seeks to balance profit with purpose, ensuring that every stakeholder reaps the benefits of its operations.

Compassionate organization begins with a clear vision that unites profitability and ethical responsibility. As I envision it, leaders in such organizations cultivate an environment where success is defined not just by financial metrics but also by the positive impact generated for all stakeholders. This vision demands fair consideration for shareholders, employees, and customers, ensuring that everyone feels valued and integral to the organization's mission. Transparency and open communication are pivotal in building trust among stakeholders, solidifying a commitment to sustainable growth that uplifts everyone involved.

Shareholders play a vital role in this equation, as their interests are aligned with sustainable and ethical business practices. Engaging shareholders in meaningful dialogue ensures that their expectations are balanced with the organization's broader social and environmental commitments. For instance, prioritizing investments in renewable energy or sustainable supply chains may entail higher upfront costs but secures long-term viability and strengthens the company's reputation. This approach underscores the interdependence between ethical practices and financial success, proving that they are not mutually exclusive goals.

Employees form the backbone of any organization, and their well-being must remain a central focus. A compassionate organization ensures that employees are fairly compensated, have access to comprehensive health benefits, and are provided with ample opportunities for professional development. Beyond material support, creating a workplace culture where employees feel respected, heard, and valued is essential. Initiatives such as flexible work arrangements, access to mental health resources, and well-defined career progression pathways enhance employees' sense of security and engagement. When employees are supported and empowered, their productivity, creativity, and commitment to the organization naturally flourish.

Leadership within a compassionate organization plays an instrumental role in exemplifying empathy and ethical responsibility. Effective leaders set the tone for the entire organization, ensuring that their actions reflect values of fairness and understanding. Training programs focused on emotional intelligence, active listening, and inclusive decision-making are crucial for cultivating leadership that inspires trust and loyalty. Leaders who genuinely care for their teams and stakeholders create an atmosphere of collaboration and respect, reinforcing the organization's cultural foundation.

Customers and consumers are integral to the organizational ecosystem, and meeting their needs with integrity is paramount. Compassionate organizations prioritize creating products and services that genuinely enhance the lives of their customers. This involves a dedication to quality, innovation, and ethical production practices. Transparent communication, ethical marketing strategies, and responsive customer service build trust and loyalty, while actively listening to customer feedback allows organizations to adapt their offerings to better align with consumer needs. These actions demonstrate the organization's unwavering commitment to providing meaningful value.

The principles of compassion extend far beyond immediate operations, encompassing corporate social responsibility. Compassionate organizations actively engage in initiatives that benefit the wider community, such as supporting education programs, funding renewable energy projects, or collaborating with nonprofits to address pressing social challenges. These efforts reflect a genuine dedication to making a positive societal impact while also strengthening the organization's reputation and building deeper connections with the community. Supporting local economies through regional sourcing, hiring local talent, and partnering with community-based initiatives further highlights the interconnection between organizational success and community well-being. Such practices not only contribute to economic growth but also deepen relationships and trust within the community.

.

Measuring success in a compassionate organization requires looking beyond conventional financial indicators. Metrics such as employee satisfaction, customer loyalty, and community impact provide a more holistic understanding of organizational effectiveness. Regular evaluations, coupled with a willingness to adapt strategies based on stakeholder feedback, ensure that the organization remains true to its core values while evolving to meet changing needs. Sharing these metrics transparently reinforces trust and accountability, showing the organization's commitment to continuous improvement and ethical practices.

Compassionate organizations have the potential to influence entire industries. By leading with ethical practices, they set a benchmark for competitors, collaborators, and partners, encouraging them to adopt similar values. This ripple effect extends across supply chains and customer behaviors, gradually developing a broader culture of responsibility and care. Educating consumers about the ethical and sustainable practices behind products further strengthens the connection between organizations and their customers. Transparency in sourcing and manufacturing processes empowers consumers to make informed choices, deepening trust and reinforcing shared values.

Technology plays an increasingly key role in compassionate organizations. Digital tools and platforms can enhance transparency, improve communication, and facilitate meaningful engagement with stakeholders. For example, technology can be used to track the environmental impact of supply chains, offering stakeholders detailed insights into the organization's sustainability practices. Additionally, using social media and digital platforms enables organizations to communicate their values and initiatives effectively, building stronger relationships with both customers and the community.

Innovation is another cornerstone of compassionate organization. Embracing innovative practices not only drives efficiency but also shows a commitment to addressing societal challenges. For instance, organizations can explore green technologies, invest in renewable energy solutions, or develop products that minimize environmental impact. Innovation nestled in compassion reflects an organization's desire to contribute positively to the world while staying competitive in the marketplace.

The importance of inclusivity cannot be overstated in compassionate organizations. By actively seeking diverse perspectives and creating spaces where all voices are heard, organizations unlock the potential for creative solutions and deeper connections. Inclusive practices ensure that decision-making processes reflect the needs and aspirations of a broad range of stakeholders, cultivating a sense of belonging and shared purpose. Workshops, employee resource groups, and community forums are just a few ways organizations can promote inclusivity and strengthen their cultural fabric.

As organizations integrate compassion into their frameworks, they must also focus on leadership development. Effective leadership programs should emphasize ethical decision-making, empathy, and long-term thinking. By equipping leaders with the skills needed to navigate complex challenges while prioritizing stakeholder well-being, organizations ensure that compassion remains a guiding principle at every level.

A Call to Action

Building a compassionate organization is not merely a goal but a necessity for long-term success. Leaders must embrace transparency, accountability, and engagement, ensuring that every decision aligns with the organization's ethical vision. Employees should feel empowered, supported, and inspired to contribute their best work. Customers and communities must experience the organization's genuine commitment to their well-being and prosperity.

To bring this vision to life, organizations must integrate compassion into every layer of their operations. From leadership development initiatives to community focused projects, every effort contributes to a culture of collaboration and care. Championing ethical practices and prioritizing meaningful contributions to society creates a positive ripple effect that benefits all stakeholders.

The future of organizational success lies in a harmonious blend of compassion and purpose. By creating environments that prioritize the well-being of people and the planet, organizations pave the way for sustainable growth, meaningful innovation, and transformative impact.

This page intentionally left blank for your reading reflection

Chapter 8

Community – Level 5
Building Together a Compassionate Community

Community is more than just a collection of people living or working together; it is the vibrant pulse of collective humanity. It transcends physical boundaries, encompassing shared values, goals, and aspirations. Communities take many forms, from neighborhoods to professional networks and digital platforms, but the essence of community remains the same: connection and collaboration.

In the framework of compassionate leadership, community plays a critical role, uniting individual efforts into collective progress. It is through cultivating a deep sense of belonging, embracing diversity, and cultivating meaningful relationships that compassionate communities thrive.

A vibrant and compassionate community begins with recognizing diversity as its strength. Each member contributes unique perspectives, skills, and experiences to the collective whole, forming a rich tapestry of ideas and solutions. Leaders in such communities embrace and celebrate this diversity, ensuring that every voice is heard and valued. The challenge lies in uniting these distinct elements into a cohesive and resilient network. This process requires intentional efforts to promote inclusivity and create spaces where individuals feel safe to express themselves and collaborate meaningfully.

Bridge-building is a cornerstone of creating unity within diversity. It involves connecting individuals and groups with varying viewpoints, cultural backgrounds, and experiences to work together toward common goals. Effective bridge-building requires deliberate actions by leaders to dismantle barriers and promote understanding. By creating opportunities for dialogue and collaboration, leaders can transform a fragmented group into a united and thriving community.

For instance, leaders can organize inclusive forums, multicultural events, or collaborative projects that encourage members to engage with one another. These initiatives allow individuals to celebrate their unique identities while recognizing the shared values that bind them. Such experiences not only break down barriers but also encourage mutual respect and trust, essential ingredients for a cohesive community.

Effective communication plays a pivotal role in bridge-building. Misunderstandings, mistrust, and cultural differences can often lead to divisions within a community. Leaders must actively promote open and empathetic communication channels, ensuring that every member feels respected and valued. Workshops on cultural sensitivity or language skills can further enhance understanding among members, strengthening their ability to work collaboratively.

Beyond encouraging unity, a compassionate community also creates a profound sense of belonging. Belonging is more than mere inclusion; it is about creating an environment where individuals feel genuinely appreciated and integral to the community's success. Leaders play a key role in cultivating this sense of belonging by recognizing and celebrating the unique contributions of each member. Inclusive decision-making processes, where diverse perspectives are actively sought and incorporated, further reinforce this sentiment. When individuals see their ideas and input reflected in the community's actions, their connection to the group deepens, and their commitment grows.

Education and awareness are essential tools for creating inclusive and compassionate communities. Leaders can design educational programs that highlight the cultural, historical, and personal narratives of their community members. These initiatives not only dismantle stereotypes but also create opportunities for meaningful connections and deeper mutual understanding. For example, workshops or seminars on cultural heritage can illuminate the diverse backgrounds of community members, seeking respect and appreciation for their unique stories.

Communities that prioritize learning and growth are better equipped to adapt to an ever-changing world. Leaders can create opportunities for lifelong learning by organizing skill-building workshops, professional development programs, and mentorship opportunities. These efforts empower individuals to expand their knowledge and contribute more effectively to the community's collective goals. Additionally, educational initiatives encourage creativity and innovation, enabling communities to find dynamic solutions to shared challenges.

Collaborative problem-solving is another hallmark of a compassionate community. By bringing together individuals with varied perspectives, experiences, and expertise, communities can address challenges with ingenuity and inclusivity. Leaders play an integral role in facilitating these collaborative efforts by creating environments where all members feel empowered to share their ideas and insights. The process not only results in innovative solutions but also builds trust and strengthens relationships within the group.

Measuring the effectiveness of a community's efforts is vital for ensuring long-term success. Leaders must establish mechanisms to evaluate engagement, cohesion, and progress within their communities. Tools such as surveys, focus groups, and feedback sessions can provide valuable insights into the needs and perceptions of members. By analyzing this data, leaders can adapt their strategies to better align with the evolving dynamics of their community. Additionally, celebrating milestones and acknowledging successes reinforces the community's collective achievements and builds a sense of pride and ownership.

Compassionate leadership within a community extends beyond addressing immediate needs; it involves advocating for systemic change to create lasting progress. Leaders must work to identify and dismantle structural barriers that hinder equity and access within their communities. This requires collaboration with local organizations, policymakers, and stakeholders to develop and implement policies that promote fairness and inclusion. By addressing systemic issues such as affordable housing, access to quality education, and healthcare, leaders demonstrate their commitment to both individual and collective well-being.

The influence of a compassionate community often extends beyond its immediate members. These communities serve as powerful examples of connection, collaboration, and inclusivity, inspiring others to adopt similar principles. The ripple effect of compassionate leadership creates networks of kindness and understanding that spread far and wide. As individuals experience the benefits of a supportive and inclusive community, they are inspired to replicate these values in their own interactions, amplifying the impact.

Technology has become an indispensable tool in modern community-building efforts. Virtual platforms, social media, and digital collaboration tools offer unprecedented opportunities for connection and engagement. Leaders can use these technologies to create inclusive and accessible spaces for dialogue, learning, and collaboration. Virtual communities transcend geographic boundaries, allowing individuals from diverse backgrounds to unite around shared interests and goals. However, the rise of digital spaces also presents challenges such as misinformation, online hostility, and digital divides. Leaders must address these issues by promoting digital literacy, cultivating respectful online interactions, and ensuring fair access to technology.

Art and culture play a transformative role in uniting communities and inspiring collective compassion. Creative expression serves as a universal language that transcends differences, encouraging empathy and connection. Leaders can integrate cultural initiatives into their community-building efforts by organizing art exhibitions, performances, and cultural festivals. These events provide opportunities for individuals to engage with one another on a deeper level, celebrating their shared humanity and diverse identities.

Intergenerational collaboration adds another dimension to compassionate community-building. By bridging the wisdom of older generations with the energy and innovation of younger members, communities can harness a wealth of knowledge and creativity. Leaders can facilitate intergenerational dialogue through mentorship programs, shared projects, and storytelling sessions. These interactions not only benefit individuals but also enhance the resilience and adaptability of the community.

The essence of community lies in its ability to create a network of support, trust, and shared purpose. Compassionate leadership strengthens this network by creating environments where individuals feel valued, empowered, and connected. By embracing diversity, encouraging collaboration, and advocating for systemic change, leaders can build communities that thrive in the face of challenges and inspire others to do the same.

Compassionate leadership is a journey that requires ongoing commitment and adaptation. As leaders and community members reflect on their roles within their networks, they must continuously seek opportunities to enhance connections and address evolving needs. Engaging with the community regularly and ensuring active participation are key to maintaining momentum and developing growth. This participatory approach transforms the community into a living, breathing entity that evolves alongside its members.

Communities flourish when individuals embrace their roles as both contributors and beneficiaries. This mutual exchange of effort and reward deepens the bonds between members and amplifies collective impact. Leaders who empower their members to take ownership of initiatives not only strengthen the community but also instill a sense of pride and purpose in its achievements. By creating opportunities for shared leadership, communities become more dynamic and resilient.

Technology continues to reshape the ways communities interact and grow. Leaders must explore innovative approaches to integrating technology into their community-building efforts. Virtual reality platforms, for instance, offer immersive experiences that bring people closer together despite geographical barriers. Social media campaigns can amplify the reach of initiatives, connecting diverse groups with common goals. By staying ahead of technological trends, leaders can ensure their communities stay relevant and engaging.

The arts and culture sector offers untapped potential for strengthening community ties. By supporting local artists and cultural events, leaders can create platforms for self-expression and connection. Public art installations and collaborative projects involving community members build a sense of ownership and pride. These initiatives can become symbols of unity, reminding everyone of the shared effort and creativity that define the community's identity.

As we reflect on the role of community in our lives, it becomes clear that we are stronger together. The connections we build within our communities extend far beyond individual relationships, creating a collective strength that propels us forward. The call to action is clear: engage with your community.

Attend local events, lend your time and skills, and support initiatives that promote unity and inclusion. Advocate for policies that address systemic barriers and create spaces where everyone feels welcome and valued. Together, we can weave a tapestry of collective compassion that transforms our neighborhoods, networks, and societies into beacons of hope and progress.

Compassionate leadership is not a finite goal but an ongoing journey. It requires dedication, empathy, and a willingness to embrace change. By committing to this journey, we can unlock the boundless potential of our communities and create a world where compassion and collaboration are at the heart of every interaction. The power of a compassionate community is immeasurable, and its impact is limited only by our willingness to lead with purpose and heart.

A Call to Action

The call to action for all of us is clear. Engage with your community. Attend local events, volunteer your time and skills, and support initiatives that promote unity and inclusion. Advocate for policies that address systemic challenges and work to create spaces where everyone feels valued and connected. By creating an environment for collective compassion, we can create a world where every community thrives, one connection at a time.

As we continue this journey of compassionate leadership, let us remember that the heart of a community lies in its people. Together, through empathy, collaboration, and shared purpose, we can transform our neighborhoods, networks, and societies into beacons of hope and progress. The power of a community is boundless, and its potential for positive change is limited only by our willingness to embrace it.

Chapter 9

Society – Level 6
Envisioning a Compassionate Future

The dream of a compassionate society transcends individual actions and extends into the collective fabric of humanity. It envisions a world where empathy, understanding, and mutual respect serve as foundational principles that guide every interaction, policy, and institution. A compassionate society nurtures and uplifts all its members, addressing disparities and creating opportunities for every individual to thrive.

A compassionate society begins with an inclusive vision, one where every person is valued, supported, and empowered to contribute meaningfully. Such a society does not merely tolerate diversity but celebrates it, recognizing that everyone's unique perspective enriches the collective. Building this society requires leaders to prioritize empathy and actively engage in creating systems that provide equitable access to resources, opportunities, and justice. Achieving this vision demands ongoing collaboration among individuals, communities, and institutions to break down barriers and cultivate an environment where everyone can flourish.

The role of political leadership in shaping societal values cannot be overstated.

When leaders embody compassion, their policies and decisions reflect this ethos. Compassionate leaders govern not just for the majority but for all citizens, with particular attention to marginalized and underserved groups. Policies designed with empathy aim to reduce systemic inequalities, combat poverty, and promote social mobility. Such leadership reflects a profound understanding that true progress is inclusive and ensures that no one is left behind.

Empathy in governance transforms decision-making. It encourages leaders to listen actively, seek diverse perspectives, and consider the long-term consequences of their choices. An empathetic approach ensures that policies are not only economically viable but also socially just and environmentally sustainable. For example, healthcare reforms prioritizing accessibility and affordability reflect a recognition of healthcare as a fundamental human right. Similarly, policies that provide universal access to education highlight the transformative power of compassion in building equitable systems. By addressing root causes, empathetic governance promotes durable solutions that create trust and social cohesion.

Social and economic equity are central to a compassionate society. Addressing disparities in wealth, education, and opportunity is not just a matter of ethics but a practical step toward creating a harmonious and prosperous community. Equitable access to resources enables individuals to contribute their talents and ideas, driving innovation and progress.

Leaders must champion initiatives that reduce these gaps, such as affordable housing programs, vocational training in underserved areas, and universal education policies. These efforts not only enhance individual potential but also strengthen the collective foundation for sustainable growth.

Community engagement is vital to cultivating a sense of belonging and shared responsibility. In a compassionate society, citizens actively take part in decision-making processes, making communities stronger and more cohesive. Encouraging such participation involves creating platforms for dialogue, ensuring transparency in governance, and empowering individuals to voice their concerns and ideas. When citizens feel their voices are heard, they are more likely to contribute meaningfully to societal progress. This empowerment can lead to transformative initiatives, such as grassroots movements and community-driven solutions to shared challenges.

The ripple effects of compassionate policies are profound. Policies that prioritize mental health contribute to a resilient and productive workforce. Education reforms focusing on inclusivity and quality empower a generation of informed and capable citizens. Public health initiatives ensuring access to clean water and nutritious food improve not only individual lives but also the overall health of communities. These policies create environments where mutual support and cooperation thrive. This cycle of positivity strengthens the social fabric, inspiring further acts of generosity and kindness.

The long-term benefits of such policies highlight the necessity of compassion as a guiding principle in governance.

The vision of a compassionate society transcends national borders. In an interconnected world, global cooperation is essential to addressing shared challenges such as climate change, pandemics, and economic inequality. Societies led by compassionate leaders are more likely to engage in collaborative efforts to tackle these issues. Such leaders recognize the well-being of one nation is intrinsically linked to the well-being of all. International initiatives that prioritize compassion, from partnerships to combat environmental degradation to global healthcare reforms, underscore the importance of solidarity in achieving lasting change. Compassionate diplomacy promotes peace and sustainability, enabling nations to work together toward shared prosperity.

Creating a compassionate society also requires confronting systemic injustices. Advocacy for fair laws, equitable representation, and inclusive policies is essential. For instance, criminal justice reforms focusing on rehabilitation rather than punishment stem from an empathetic understanding of the root causes of crime. Similarly, investments in workforce development and education for underserved populations show a commitment to breaking cycles of poverty and promoting upward mobility. Addressing systemic challenges demands continuous effort and adaptability.

Leaders must remain attuned to evolving societal needs, ensuring policies align with the principles of equity and justice. While leadership and policy play significant roles, the foundation of a compassionate society lies in the actions of its citizens. Everyday acts of kindness, volunteering, and support for local initiatives contribute to a culture of care and solidarity. These actions reinforce the values of empathy and cooperation that underpin a compassionate society.

Individuals can drive meaningful changes at the local level through initiatives such as mentoring programs, neighborhood improvement projects, and grassroots advocacy. These seemingly small efforts inspire others and create a cascading effect of positive impact, amplifying the network of compassion and support within communities.

Education is a powerful catalyst for cultivating compassion. Schools and educational institutions are the bedrock for nurturing empathy and understanding among future generations. Curricula emphasizing social and emotional learning, cultural awareness, and ethical decision-making prepare students to engage with the world thoughtfully and compassionately. Programs encouraging community service or cross-cultural exchanges deepen students' understanding of global interconnectedness and shared responsibility.

A compassionate educational approach prioritizes constructive feedback and support, helping students build resilience and a growth mindset. By instilling these values early, education lays the groundwork for a society where empathy and cooperation are integral to every interaction.

Art and culture also play a transformative role in cultivating compassion within societies. Through storytelling, music, visual arts, and theater, communities can explore complex emotions and bridge cultural divides. Cultural initiatives that bring people together to share traditions and experiences promote unity and mutual respect. Art's unique ability to touch hearts and minds inspires individuals to embrace compassion in their interactions and decisions. Public art installations, performances, and cultural festivals provide opportunities for connection and expression, enriching the social fabric and reinforcing shared humanity.

The journey toward a compassionate society requires a collective commitment from leaders and citizens alike. Prioritizing the collective well-being over individual gain, embracing diversity, and working collaboratively to create fair systems are essential steps. Each act of compassion, whether large or small, contributes to the collective strength of society, bringing us closer to achieving this vision. The path may be challenging, but the rewards of a society built on empathy and understanding are immeasurable.

A Call to Action

As we move forward, let us remember that the foundation of a compassionate society lies in our willingness to connect, collaborate, and care for one another. Leaders must commit to creating policies that address disparities and prioritize collective well-being. Citizens, too, have an essential role in advocating for equity and practicing empathy in daily interactions. Attend local events, support community-driven initiatives, and use your voice to advocate for systemic change. By embracing these principles, we can transform our communities and create a brighter future for all.

Together, we can ensure that compassion guides our shared journey, leaving a legacy of hope, justice, and equity for generations to come. Creating compassionate leaders and compassionate societies begins with each of us, and its impact will echo across time, shaping a world where every individual can thrive.

This page intentionally left blank for your reading reflection

_____

_____

_____

_____

_____

_____

_____

_____

_____

_____

_____

_____

Chapter 10

Serving Others – Level 7
The Compassionate Noble Leader

The ultimate expression of leadership transcends personal ambition, status, or gain. It delves into the profound realm of selfless service, where the leader's purpose becomes an unwavering commitment to uplifting others and shaping a better world. This chapter explores the transformative journey toward embodying the virtues of a compassionate noble leader, one who integrates empathy, integrity, and a deep sense of responsibility to serve humanity without expectation of anything in return.

True leadership begins with a clear and unwavering vision of selfless service. Compassionate-noble leaders see leadership not as a pursuit of power or prestige but as a platform to effect meaningful change. They prioritize the well-being of others above personal accolades, finding fulfillment in acts of generosity, justice, and care. For these leaders, success is not defined by authority or recognition but by the impact they have on those they serve. This vision serves as the guiding principle for compassionate leadership, anchoring all decisions and actions in a desire to contribute positively to humanity.

Central to compassionate-noble leadership is the art of giving without expectation. The most profound acts of leadership are those performed selflessly and with humility. Leaders who embody this principle understand that the value of their contributions lies not in external validation but in the positive change they inspire. Whether mentoring emerging professionals, supporting colleagues during tough times, or championing meaningful causes, such leaders stay focused on creating value for others. This approach transforms leadership into a quiet yet powerful force for good, emphasizing the importance of meaningful action over public recognition.

The influence of selfless service extends beyond the individual leader. Compassionate-noble leaders inspire those around them to adopt similar values, creating environments characterized by collaboration, empathy, and mutual support. These leaders model selflessness, showing that leadership is most effective when it is centered on collective well-being. In workplaces, schools, and communities, this ripple effect creates cultures that prioritize care, integrity, and shared progress. By cultivating selflessness in others, leaders amplify their impact, enabling broader and more lasting change.

Creating a culture of selflessness requires intentional effort. Compassionate leaders actively provide opportunities for others to engage in acts of service. Whether through community projects, employee-led initiatives, or mentorship programs, these opportunities empower individuals to contribute to causes aligned with their values. Such platforms not only enable meaningful contributions but also strengthen the collective ethos of compassion within organizations and communities. By prioritizing these initiatives, leaders help set up networks of support that extend far beyond their immediate influence.

Walking the path of selfless service is not without its challenges. Compassionate leaders often face skepticism, resistance, and adversity, assessing their resolve and commitment to their values. However, these challenges provide opportunities for growth and reaffirmation of purpose. By practicing continuous self-reflection, humility, and resilience, leaders can navigate these obstacles with grace. They remain steadfast in their dedication to serving others, finding strength in their belief in compassion and the transformative power of selfless leadership.

Despite the difficulties, the fulfillment derived from selfless service is unmatched. Compassionate noble leaders experience a profound sense of joy and purpose in knowing that their actions have positively impacted others. This fulfillment transcends material rewards, offering a deeply satisfying reminder of why they chose this path. The contentment that comes from giving freely and wholeheartedly reinforces the belief that true leadership is about elevating and inspiring others. It is this intrinsic reward that sustains compassionate leaders on their journey.

Compassionate noble leadership challenges conventional definitions of success. Instead of measuring achievements by wealth, power, or accolades, it encourages leaders to assess their impact through the lives they touch and the positive change they create. This redefined vision of success elevates leadership to a higher purpose, emphasizing service over self-interest. By embracing this perspective, leaders set a powerful example, inspiring others to prioritize humanity's collective well-being over personal ambition.

True success lies in building a community of leaders who share a vision of selfless service. Compassionate-noble leaders understand the value of mentorship and empowerment, recognizing that their impact is multiplied when others adopt and carry forward these principles. By creating a culture of shared values and mutual support, these leaders lay the foundation for enduring change. The legacy of compassionate leadership is not confined to a single individual but is perpetuated by the collective efforts of those inspired to serve.

Integrity is the backbone of compassionate leadership. It ensures that actions align with ethical principles and that decisions are guided by fairness and transparency. Leaders who uphold integrity inspire trust, build stronger relationships and more cohesive communities. This unwavering commitment to ethical conduct reinforces the foundation of selfless service, ensuring that the leader's vision remains clear and their influence enduring. Integrity is not just a principle; it is the essence of credibility and respect in leadership.

The challenges of leadership are often dynamic and unpredictable, requiring compassionate leaders to embrace adaptability. By remaining open to feedback, reflecting on experiences, and striving for continuous improvement, leaders enhance their ability to navigate complexities effectively. Adaptability ensures that their actions remain aligned with the principles of compassion, even in the face of evolving circumstances. It is this flexibility that allows leaders to respond creatively and confidently to new challenges, keeping their commitment to selfless service.

Empathy is a cornerstone of compassionate leadership, enabling leaders to connect deeply with others and understand their perspectives, challenges, and needs. By prioritizing empathy, leaders create environments where trust, collaboration, and mutual understanding thrive. Whether in one-on-one interactions or broader organizational practices, empathy enhances decision-making and strengthens relationships. Compassionate leaders recognize that empathy is not just a skill but a vital element of meaningful and informed leadership.

The impact of compassionate leadership extends far beyond individual actions. Leaders who prioritize selfless service inspire others to do the same, creating a culture of generosity and collaboration that benefits entire communities. This ripple effect drives tangible progress, addressing systemic issues such as poverty, inequality, and environmental sustainability. By championing compassion and service, leaders contribute to a collective legacy of positive change, improving outcomes for all.

The principles of compassionate-noble leadership have the potential to transform entire systems and structures. By embedding compassion, integrity, and empathy into the fabric of organizations and communities, leaders create environments that prioritize the well-being of all members. This transformation requires a commitment to continuous learning, collaboration, and a shared sense of purpose. Through these efforts, the legacy of selfless service endures, shaping a world where compassion is the cornerstone of progress.

Small acts of kindness hold immense power. A word of encouragement, a gesture of support, or a willingness to listen can create lasting change and inspire others. These moments of compassion reinforce the idea that leadership is not about grand displays of power but about the consistent practice of uplifting others. Each act contributes to a culture of care and understanding, magnifying the collective impact of compassionate leadership.

The journey of compassionate leadership is a profound and rewarding endeavor. It challenges leaders to rise above personal ambitions and embrace the higher purpose of serving others. This path informs, inspires, and transforms both the leader and those they serve. By embodying the virtues of a compassionate-noble leader, individuals have the power to illuminate the way forward, leaving a legacy of care, understanding, and unwavering commitment to humanity's betterment.

A Call to Action

The call to action is clear: embrace the principles of selfless service and compassionate leadership. Let your vision of leadership transcend personal ambition, focusing instead on the impact you can create in the lives of others. Invest in building communities of care, integrity, and empathy. Commit to continuous growth and inspire those around you to do the same. Together, we can create a future defined by shared humanity, enduring hope, and boundless compassion. Each act of service contributes to a collective legacy, shaping a world where leadership is synonymous with care, integrity, and purpose.

This page intentionally left blank for your reading reflection

Chapter 11

Comparison of Leadership Models
Comparing Compassionate Leadership to Other Models

Leadership has long been the cornerstone of human progress, with numerous models and approaches shaping how individuals, organizations, and societies navigate change, achieve goals, and address challenges. Among these models, compassionate leadership stands apart as a transformative approach that not only achieves tangible results but also develops well-being, inclusivity, and a shared sense of purpose. Central to this approach is the Compassionate Leadership Pyramid and Model, which integrates the best practices of existing leadership styles into a cohesive framework for personal and societal transformation.

Authoritarian "Centralized-Autocratic" Leadership

Authoritarian leadership centralizes decision-making power in the leader, often emphasizing efficiency and control. While this model may be effective in crisis situations, it often stifles creativity, engagement, and morale. Compassionate leadership offers an alternative by cultivating collaboration, autonomy, and shared accountability, resulting in more resilient and innovative teams. Within the Pyramid, this is a shift from control to empowerment, where leaders guide rather than dictate, enabled by self-awareness and mindful leadership.

Democratic "Decentralized" Leadership

Democratic leadership emphasizes collective decision-making and values the input of team members. While this model promotes inclusivity and engagement, it can sometimes be inefficient or indecisive in high-pressure situations. Compassionate leadership integrates the inclusivity of democratic approaches with decisive action grounded in empathy and a clear vision, striking a balance between collaboration and effective leadership. This level of the Pyramid emphasizes shared purpose and inclusive decision-making, underpinned by the leader's mindful approach to navigating diverse perspectives.

Flexible Leadership

Flexible leadership is defined by adaptability and responsiveness, allowing leaders to adjust their style and strategies based on situational needs. It integrates elements from various leadership models, striking a balance between task-oriented and people-focused approaches. This pragmatism makes flexible leadership highly effective in fast-changing environments or when addressing diverse challenges. While it excels in its ability to respond dynamically, it may lack the deep emotional grounding of compassionate leadership. It is less suitable for situations requiring sustained trust and emotional connection.

Compassionate leadership is most impactful in situations requiring long-term cultural change, trust-building, and emotional investment. Flexible leadership shines in dynamic environments where adaptability is essential. Each model has unique strengths, and the choice should align with the specific goals, challenges, and cultural needs of the organization or group.

Kleptocratic Leadership

Kleptocratic leadership and compassionate leadership represent two fundamentally opposing approaches to leadership. Compassionate leadership is rooted in empathy, connection, and service to others, nurturing trust and promoting growth by prioritizing the well-being of individuals and communities. It creates environments of fairness, collaboration, and shared success, inspiring positive change and empowering others to thrive.

In stark contrast, kleptocratic leadership is centered on greed, corruption, and the pursuit of personal gain at the expense of people and systems. It erodes trust, exploits power for selfish ends, and encourages inequality and dysfunction, leaving organizations and societies in disarray.

The choice between these models defines the impact a leader has on those they serve. Compassionate leadership builds legacies of integrity, progress, and resilience, while kleptocratic leadership leaves a trail of destruction and harm. This contrast underscores the critical need for ethical and compassionate governance in shaping a better future.

Servant Leadership

Servant leadership emphasizes the leader's role as a steward of their followers' needs, prioritizing service over authority. While it shares similarities with compassionate leadership, such as a focus on humility and service, servant leadership can sometimes lack the structured framework to drive large-scale systemic change. Compassionate leadership integrates the selflessness of servant leadership with strategic vision, enabling leaders to address individual needs while affecting broader organizational or societal transformation. In the Pyramid, this reflects the "service others" level, connecting altruism with action and reinforced by a leader's deep self-awareness.

Situational Leadership

Situational leadership is adaptable, with leaders modifying their style to suit the needs of their team and the context. While this flexibility is valuable, it can sometimes result in inconsistency or lack of authenticity. Compassionate leadership incorporates situational awareness but anchors it in a consistent ethos of empathy and care, ensuring that adaptability does not come at the cost of trust and relational depth. This adaptability forms the dynamic level "ascend and descend" of the Pyramid, where responsiveness meets rooted compassion, informed by a mindful presence. Leaders operating at the Society level might recognize the need for greater self-compassion. In such cases, they can step down to that foundational level, focus on improvement and growth, and then rise back to their original level with renewed strength and understanding.

Soft Leadership

Compassionate leadership emphasizes serving others selflessly, building trust, and prioritizing the well-being of individuals and communities. Rooted in mindfulness and self-awareness, it seeks to create a nurturing environment that values empathy and collaborative decision-making.

This model is particularly effective in scenarios where emotional intelligence and the ability to address complex interpersonal dynamics are critical. By contrast, soft leadership, while also people-oriented, focuses on persuasion, nurturing relationships, and influencing others through care and emotional connection. It is less structured than compassionate leadership and often prioritizes harmony and morale over transformative change, making it suitable for environments needing relationship building over direct action. It may lack the structure and goal-driven focus of other leadership models, making it less effective in high-pressure or goal-intensive situations. However, it works best in nurturing collaborative teams where harmony and emotional engagement are primary goals.

Transactional Leadership

Transactional leadership relies on structured systems of rewards and punishments to manage performance and achieve goals. While it is effective in environments that require clear directives and consistency, this model can overlook the human dimension of leadership. Compassionate leadership transcends transactional approaches by prioritizing relationships, intrinsic motivation, and the holistic wellbeing of followers, creating a more sustainable and fulfilling dynamic. This approach fits into the operational layer of the Pyramid, where clear expectations meet human connection, guided by an empathetic understanding enhanced through mindfulness.

Transformational Leadership

Transformational leadership focuses on inspiring and motivating followers to achieve extraordinary outcomes. Leaders in this model emphasize vision, innovation, and personal development. While transformational leadership is highly effective in driving change and encouraging engagement, it often prioritizes results over relational well-being. Compassionate leadership encompasses the transformative aspects of this model but balances them with empathy and attention to the emotional and social needs of individuals. Within the Compassionate Leadership Pyramid, this forms the layer where vision aligns with values, anchored in mindfulness and self-awareness.

As we explore together, what sets compassionate leadership apart is its ability to encompass and enhance the strengths of other models while addressing their limitations. By prioritizing empathy, altruism, and shared humanity, compassionate leadership ensures that both goals and relationships are given equal weight. This integrative approach creates a framework that is adaptable, sustainable, and deeply impactful.

Visionary like Transformational Leadership: Compassionate leaders inspire and motivate by articulating a vision that resonates with shared values and aspirations.

Accountable like Transactional Leadership: They set clear expectations and hold themselves and others accountable, but always within a framework of care and support.

Selfless like Servant Leadership: Compassionate leaders prioritize the needs of others while maintaining the ability to make strategic decisions that benefit the collective.

Adaptable like Situational Leadership: They adjust their approach to suit the context but remain anchored in empathy and integrity.

Collaborative like Democratic Leadership: Compassionate leaders create inclusion and engagement, ensuring that every voice is heard and valued.

Resilient in Crisis: Unlike authoritarian leaders, who rely on control, compassionate leaders leverage trust and unity to navigate crises effectively.

The Role of Mindfulness and Self-Awareness

At the heart of compassionate leadership mindfulness and self-awareness, form the foundation upon which all other elements rest. These core practices enable leaders to connect deeply with themselves and others, cultivating clarity, empathy, and resilience. Compassionate leadership is not just a method but a way of being, one that acknowledges humanity in every interaction and prioritizes collective growth over individual gain. They enable leaders to:

- **Recognize** their own biases, emotions, and triggers, allowing for more intentional and thoughtful decision-making.
- **Cultivate** a sense of presence, ensuring they are fully engaged in every interaction.
- **Develop** resilience to navigate challenges with clarity and composure.

- **Cultivate** empathy by understanding their own experiences and extending that understanding to others.

These practices transform leadership from a set of actions to a way of being, creating a ripple effect that inspires trust, collaboration, and collective growth.

A Call to Action for Leaders

The challenges of our era demand leaders who can navigate complexity while staying grounded in humanity. Compassionate leadership is not merely an ideal but a necessity for cultivating resilient organizations and stable peaceful societies. Leaders at every level of the pyramid are called to embrace this model, integrating empathy and compassion into their decision-making and interactions.

To adopt compassionate leadership, start with self-awareness and mindfulness. Understand your values, biases, and emotional triggers. Cultivate empathy by actively listening and looking to understand the experiences of others. Prioritize relationships and invest in creating environments where people feel valued, supported, and empowered.

Compassionate leadership is a journey, not a destination. It requires continuous growth, reflection, and a commitment to serving others. As leaders, the impact we create extends far beyond our immediate spheres, shaping the cultures, communities, and systems of which we are a part. By embracing the principles of compassionate leadership, we can build a world where kindness, justice, and shared prosperity prevail.

Among the myriad leadership models, compassionate leadership stands out as the most holistic and transformative. It not only achieves results but also uplifts individuals and communities, creating a legacy of empathy and altruism. By integrating the strengths of other approaches and addressing their limitations, compassionate leadership emerges as the ideal framework for navigating the complexities of our modern world. Anchored in mindfulness and self-awareness, it empowers leaders to elevate those around them while building a future defined by unity, hope, and shared purpose.

Chapter 12

Turning Data into Insights
Revealing the Power of
Compassionate Leadership

The development and validation of the Compassionate Leadership Model relied heavily on research conducted over an 18-month period, from May 2021 to November 2022. This extensive study involved a diverse sample of participants across industries, allowing for a nuanced understanding of how leadership practices impact individuals' attitudes, behaviors, and willingness to serve others. This chapter delves into the process of turning raw data into actionable insights and explores the implications of these findings for academics, practitioners, and organizations striving to cultivate compassionate leadership.

Research Design and Methodology

The study utilized a mixed-methods approach, incorporating questionnaires, surveys, and observations to collect data. Participants represented various industries, cultural backgrounds, and hierarchical levels within organizations. The goal was to capture a comprehensive picture of how leadership practices influence individuals' propensity for compassionate behavior and their willingness to serve others.

By analyzing both qualitative and quantitative data, the study identified patterns, trends, and key variables that contribute to compassionate leadership. The findings serve as a foundation for understanding the mechanisms through which leadership can cultivate empathy, compassion, and collaboration within teams and organizations.

Key Insights from Research:

The Role of Culture in Compassionate Leadership

One of the most striking findings was the impact of organizational and societal culture on individuals' willingness to serve others. **Seventy percent (70%)** of participants showed that the culture set by leaders significantly shapes their attitudes and behaviors. This underscores the pivotal role of leadership in establishing values and norms that promote compassion within organizations.

When leaders prioritize empathy, inclusiveness, and mutual respect, these values permeate the organization, creating an environment where individuals feel motivated to help and support one another. Cultures characterized by competition, hierarchy, or neglect of employee well-being may stifle compassionate behavior, leading to disengagement and reduced collaboration.

The Influence of Natural Compassionate Leaders

Approximately **4%** of individuals in the study were identified as natural compassionate leaders—individuals who innately show empathy, compassion and a genuine concern for others. These individuals play a critical role in their teams and organizations, serving as catalysts for positive change and role models for compassionate behavior. Their presence highlights the value of recognizing and nurturing these innate qualities. Organizations and societies can amplify their impact by providing these leaders with platforms to mentor others, influence decision-making, and shape organizational culture in meaningful ways.

Addressing Negative Experiences

Not all participants had a positive journey toward serving others. The study found that **12%** of individuals had been discouraged by negative experiences, such as lack of recognition, unsupportive environments, or failures in past efforts to help others. These setbacks often lead to disillusionment, reducing their willingness to engage in compassionate acts.

Organizations must acknowledge and address these barriers to create a more supportive environment. This can include providing constructive feedback, celebrating acts of compassion, and creating spaces where individuals feel safe to take risks and learn from failures. By addressing these challenges, organizations can help individuals regain their confidence and motivation to serve.

Overcoming a Lack of Concern for Others

A significant challenge identified in the study was the **8%** of individuals who exhibited a lack of concern for others and a reluctance to help. This group represents a critical area for intervention, as their attitudes can negatively influence team dynamics and organizational culture.

To engage these individuals, organizations may need to employ targeted strategies such as empathy training, exposure to collaborative projects, and initiatives that show the tangible benefits of compassion. By gradually shifting their mindset, these individuals can begin to see the value of compassionate leadership for both personal and organizational success.

Activating Passive Participants

Another group highlighted by the study was the 6% of individuals who adopted a passive approach to compassion. While not overtly resistant, these individuals often fail to take initiative in serving others or contributing to organizational goals.

To activate their potential, organizations can provide structured opportunities for involvement, such as volunteer programs, team-building exercises, or leadership development workshops. Empowering these individuals with specific roles and responsibilities can help them transition from passive observers to active contributors.

Practical Applications of the Insights

The findings of this research offer actionable guidance for leaders, HR professionals, and organizational designers looking to embed compassion into their practices and policies. Here are key strategies for turning these insights into impactful actions:

Cultivating Compassionate Cultures

Leaders should recognize their influence in shaping organizational culture and actively model compassionate behavior. This involves showing empathy in decision-making, prioritizing employee well-being, and celebrating acts of kindness and collaboration.

Clear communication of organizational values, combined with consistent actions, reinforces a culture of compassion. Leaders can also set up programs that reward and recognize compassionate behaviors, creating a positive feedback loop that encourages more individuals to engage in these practices.

Nurturing Natural Leaders

Identifying natural compassionate leaders within the organization is essential. These individuals can be empowered through leadership development programs, mentorship opportunities, and roles that amplify their impact.

By positioning natural leaders as ambassadors of compassion, organizations can use their influence to inspire others, shape policies, and drive initiatives that align with the values of empathy and service.

Rebuilding Confidence After Negative Experiences

For individuals discouraged by past setbacks, organizations must provide avenues for rebuilding confidence. This includes creating supportive environments where mistakes are viewed as "learning opportunities" rather than failures.

Leaders can play a pivotal role by offering constructive feedback, celebrating progress, and showing patience and understanding. Encouraging open dialogue about challenges and solutions encourages resilience and a renewed willingness to serve others.

Encouraging Engagement and Active Participation

To address passivity and lack of engagement, organizations should design initiatives that are both accessible and impactful. Providing clear roles, resources, and support enables individuals to contribute meaningfully without feeling overwhelmed or uncertain.

Structured programs, such as team-based volunteer projects or collaborative innovation challenges, can motivate individuals to step out of their comfort zones and actively participate in compassionate initiatives.

Implications for Future Research and Practice

The insights derived from this study represent a starting point for deeper exploration into the mechanisms and outcomes of compassionate leadership. Future research could explore other variables, such as cultural differences, industry-specific challenges, and long-term impacts on organizational performance. Practitioners can also experiment with innovative approaches to leadership development, incorporating findings from this study to encourage tailored programs that address the unique needs of their teams and organizations. By continuously refining these practices, organizations can build a pipeline of compassionate leaders ready to tackle the challenges of tomorrow.

Transforming Data into Impact

By understanding the dynamics of culture, innate qualities, and individual challenges, organizations can implement targeted strategies to cultivate empathy, collaboration, and service-oriented mindsets.

Turning data into insights is only the first step. The true impact lies in translating these insights into actions that inspire individuals, strengthen organizations, and create a more compassionate and connected world. As we move forward, the principles of compassionate leadership serve as both a guide and a challenge, calling on leaders to embrace empathy as a cornerstone of their practice and a catalyst for lasting change.

Chapter 13

Consequences and Benefits of Compassionate Leadership

Compassionate leadership is more than a philosophy; it is a transformative approach that extends far beyond the immediate individuals, groups, teams, and organizations.

Positive Consequences: By prioritizing empathy, inclusiveness, compassion and mutual respect, compassionate leaders create environments that encourage collaboration, diversity, and authentic expression. This section explores the profound impacts of compassionate leadership, highlighting its ability to shape organizational cultures, enhance workforce engagement, and unlock collective potential.

The behaviors and values modeled by compassionate leaders inspire others to adopt similar approaches, creating a ripple effect that spreads empathy and collaboration throughout the workplace and beyond. This ripple effect creates a more inclusive and fair society, as organizations led by compassionate leaders prioritize social responsibility, ethical practices, community engagement, and corporate responsibility. Compassionate leadership creates environments where trust, collaboration, and mutual respect thrive, leading to healthier workplaces, stronger communities, and a more collaborative global economy. Research highlights that this approach improves employee satisfaction, retention, and performance while enhancing innovation and adaptability. These outcomes are the natural result of prioritizing empathy and compassion, as shown in the Compassionate Leadership Model and Pyramid.

Negative Consequences: In contrast, leadership models that prioritize results over relationships lacks compassion in leadership, which often lead to negative consequences such as burnout, disengagement, and toxic cultures. Employees in these environments may feel undervalued, resulting in decreased productivity and high turnover. Similarly, societies led by leaders who lack compassion can face deeper social divides, inequities, and unrest.

Collaboration as a Cornerstone of Success

One of the most significant outcomes of compassionate leadership is the promotion of collaboration. Compassionate leaders create an atmosphere where individuals feel valued, respected, and supported, encouraging open communication and trust.

In such an environment, teams and groups move beyond competition to embrace cooperation, aligning their efforts towards shared goals.

The shift from competition to collaboration enables individuals to pool their strengths and resources, resulting in greater efficiency and effectiveness. Compassionate leaders cultivate this spirit of teamwork by encouraging mutual support and emphasizing the collective success of the group over individual achievements. This approach strengthens relationships, enhances problem-solving capabilities, and encourages collaboration as a cornerstone of both individual and organizational success.

The Benefits of Compassionate Leadership

Compassionate leadership is not just a noble ideal, it is a practical and transformative approach with far-reaching benefits for individuals, teams, organizations, and society. By prioritizing empathy, emotional intelligence, and the well-being of others, compassionate leaders create environments where people thrive, relationships strengthen, and innovation flourish.

Enhanced Employee Well-Being: Compassionate leaders help create supportive environments where employees feel valued and respected. This focus on care and empathy reduces stress, improves mental health, and enhances job satisfaction. Employees who feel secure and supported are more engaged, motivated, and resilient, leading to lower absenteeism and burnout rates.

Increased Productivity and Performance:

When employees feel appreciated and trusted, they are more likely to take ownership of their work and strive for excellence. Compassionate leadership encourages open communication, collaboration, and accountability, empowering teams to innovate, solve problems, and achieve ambitious goals. This translates to stronger individual and organizational outcomes.

Strengthened Relationships and Team Cohesion:

Compassionate leadership builds trust and mutual respect within teams. By prioritizing relational well-being, leaders help create a sense of unity and collaboration. Employees feel comfortable sharing ideas, giving feedback, and supporting one another, resulting in stronger team dynamics and deeper loyalty between leaders and their teams.

Enhanced Innovation and Creativity: By creating a culture of psychological safety, compassionate leaders inspire employees to take risks, share ideas, and explore new possibilities. Embracing diverse perspectives and treating mistakes as opportunities for growth unlocks the collective potential of teams, driving creativity and positioning organizations to thrive in dynamic environments.

Improved Employee Engagement and Retention: Employees who feel valued and supported are more engaged, committed, and loyal. Compassionate leadership inspires a sense of purpose and connection, reducing turnover and encouraging a stable, high-performing workforce. This investment in people not only enhances organizational success but also reduces costs associated with employee turnover.

Positive Organizational Culture: Compassionate leaders set the tone for a culture rooted in empathy, respect, and inclusivity. This foundation encourages collaboration, trust, and mutual support, creating an environment where individuals and teams can excel. A compassionate culture attracts top talent, strengthens the organization's reputation, and embeds ethical decision-making and social responsibility into the workplace.

Embracing Diversity of Thoughts and Ideas: Compassionate leaders recognize the value of diversity and inclusion, understanding that varied perspectives drive innovation and effective problem-solving. By creating an environment where individuals feel safe expressing their unique viewpoints, leaders tap into the collective intelligence of their teams. This inclusivity builds respect, strengthens team dynamics, and enhances organizational success.

Broader Societal Impact: The influence of compassionate leadership extends beyond the workplace. Organizations led by compassionate leaders often engage in socially responsible practices, support community initiatives, and advocate for equity and sustainability. Employees who experience compassion at work carry those values into their personal lives, contributing to stronger communities and a more just and empathetic society.

Building Resilience and Adaptability: Compassionate leaders help teams navigate challenges and uncertainties with confidence by providing support and understanding. This approach develops resilience and a growth mindset, enabling teams to embrace change and seize opportunities for innovation. In today's rapidly evolving world, this adaptability is essential for long-term success.

Embracing the Transformative Power of Compassionate Leadership

Compassionate leadership is more than a leadership style, it is a catalyst for positive change. By embracing empathy, compassion, encouraging collaboration, and creating cultures of trust and inclusivity, compassionate leaders drive innovation, resilience, and societal progress. Their influence shapes not only the organizations they lead but also the communities and societies they touch, leaving a legacy of care and progress for generations to come.

At its core, compassionate leadership begins with self-awareness and mindfulness, cultivating resilience and a deep understanding of personal values. From this foundation, it extends outward, strengthening relationships, encouraging collaboration, and building healthier communities and ethical organizations. Compassionate leaders challenge the status quo by prioritizing the well-being of their teams, stakeholders, and society, recognizing that true success is measured by the positive impact they create.

A Leadership Style That Inspires Transformation

Compassionate leadership promotes collaboration by creating environments where individuals feel valued, respected, and supported. Trust, open communication, and inclusivity thrive under this approach, enabling teams to align their efforts toward shared goals. This shift from competition to cooperation enhances problem-solving capabilities, builds stronger relationships, and unlocks the potential of individuals and organizations.

Empathy and compassion are at the heart of compassionate leadership. Empathy enables leaders to understand the perspectives and needs of others, breaking down barriers and encouraging a sense of belonging. Compassion drives leaders to prioritize collective success over personal gain, using their influence to serve a greater purpose. Together, these principles build trust, drive innovation, and create cultures rooted in mutual care and respect.

The influence of compassionate leadership extends far beyond the workplace. Organizations led by compassionate leaders prioritize social responsibility, ethical practices, corporate responsibility and community engagement. This creates a cascading impact, enabling stronger communities, more fair societies, and a more collaborative global economy.

Compassionate leaders inspire those around them to act with empathy and generosity, creating cultures where acts of kindness are celebrated, and trust is built. This ripple effect empowers individuals, strengthens teams, and drives systemic change. By addressing root causes of inequality and promoting justice, compassionate leadership unites diverse groups and builds a shared vision for the future.

A Call to Action for Leaders

The challenges we face today, social injustice, economic inequality, environmental crises, demand a new approach to leadership. Compassionate leadership offers a pathway toward unity and understanding by placing humanity at the forefront. Leaders are called to embrace compassion as a guiding principle, letting empathy inform decisions and compassion shape actions.

Compassionate leadership is not without its challenges. It requires courage, resilience, and a willingness to confront difficult truths. Yet, the rewards far outweigh the obstacles. By encouraging collaboration, diversity, and inclusion, compassionate leaders help create environments where trust and respect thrive, unlocking the potential for sustainable success.

The Future Belongs to Compassionate Leadership

Organizations embracing compassionate leadership lay the foundation for a future defined by empathy, compassion, innovation, and shared prosperity. This approach delivers measurable benefits, from enhanced employee well-being and productivity to stronger relationships and a positive organizational culture. It empowers individuals, transforms communities, and inspires a collective commitment to the greater good.

As compassionate leadership continues to shape individuals, organizations, and societies, it emerges as a powerful force for positive change. By embracing this approach, leaders not only transform those they lead but also leave a legacy of hope, humanity, and a better world for all.

This page intentionally left blank for your reading reflection

---

Chapter 14

The Journey of
Compassionate Leadership
A Call to Action for All

As we have explored so far, compassionate leadership is a transformative force that has the power to create a brighter and more fair future. It is not just a philosophy but a practical approach that calls on individuals, organizations, and communities to embrace empathy and compassion as guiding principles. Together, we can shape a world where kindness, understanding, and justice prevail, where every step toward compassion strengthens the foundation for meaningful change.

How Do I Start?

For **individuals** and **aspiring leaders**, the journey begins with self-reflection. Understand your values, strengths, and areas for growth. Cultivate self-awareness and mindfulness while committing to continuous learning. Surround yourself with diverse perspectives and seek opportunities to practice empathy and compassion. Leadership is a journey, not a destination, every step you take toward compassion brings you closer to your full human potential.

For **organizations**, the path begins with creating cultures of compassion and inclusion. Invest in leadership development programs that emphasize empathy, ethics, and equity. Create environments where employees feel valued, empowered, and supported. Align your mission with social responsibility and advocate for positive change. By embedding compassion into your organizational DNA, you can drive innovation, resilience, and long-term success.

For **communities and society**, the call is to champion compassionate leadership. Celebrate leaders who show empathy and integrity, and support policies that promote inclusivity and sustainability. Encourage collaboration across sectors to address shared challenges, using collective action for systemic change.

Where Do We Go from Here? Advancing the Seven Levels of Compassionate Leadership

As the Compassionate Leadership Pyramid unfolds, it offers a roadmap for transformative impact. Each level deepens the practice of compassion, guiding leaders to expand their influence from self-awareness to societal change.

Self-Compassion (Level 1): Begin by cultivating self-awareness and mindfulness. Reflect on your values, emotions, and areas for growth to build resilience and clarity. By prioritizing your well-being, you prepare to support others effectively.

Next of Kin – Compassion for Your Own Tribe **(Level 2):** Strengthen bonds with family and close relationships (inner circles). Practice active listening, gratitude, and support to build trust and stability that enable you to face broader challenges.

Local Environment (Level 3): Engage with your local community by volunteering, supporting local initiatives, or participating in civic activities. Your presence and efforts create tangible, meaningful impacts that inspire others.

Organization – Organizational Impact (Level 4): Act with integrity and empathy within your workplace. Develop and encourage inclusivity, fair practices, and wellbeing for employees. Small actions, like mentoring or supporting team initiatives, create lasting positive change.

Community – Community Engagement (Level 5): Use your voice to amplify causes that align with your values. Collaborate with others to address shared challenges, strengthen the social fabric, and create solutions that benefit all.

Society – Societal Influence (Level 6): Advocate for systemic change by addressing inequities and promoting sustainability. Use your influence to inspire others to adopt compassionate principles, reshaping societal norms and practices.

Serving Others – The Compassionate Leader (Level 7): Embrace selfless service as the pinnacle of compassionate leadership. Dedicate yourself to the well-being of others without expectation of personal gain, creating a legacy of compassion that inspires generations.

Your Role in the Journey

Compassionate leadership is for everyone, regardless of position or sphere of influence. Reflect on where you are within the seven levels of the pyramid and take action from there:

- Start with self-compassion to build resilience.
- Strengthen your inner circle to create a foundation of trust.
- Engage with your local environment to inspire positive change.
- Contribute to your organization by encouraging fairness and empathy.
- Connect with the broader community to amplify causes and collaborate on solutions.
- Advocate for societal change to address inequities and promote sustainability.
- Embrace selfless service to create a lasting legacy of compassion.

A Vision for the Future

Compassionate leadership is not the domain of a select few; it is a universal call to action. By embracing the principles of the Compassionate

Leadership Model and Pyramid, individuals, organizations, and communities can work together to create a world where everyone has the opportunity to thrive. This journey requires courage, resilience, and unwavering dedication, but the rewards, both personal and collective, are immeasurable.

Together, we can build a legacy of compassion that transforms our world for generations to come.

Together We Can Make It Happen

The path and journey forward depend on our collective action. While compassionate leadership starts with individuals, its impact multiplies when embraced by communities, organizations, and societies. Your role is to carry this message forward, to practice compassion in your daily life and inspire others to do the same.

Compassionate leadership is not about perfection; it is about progress. Each step you take toward empathy and compassion contributes to a brighter future. Together, we can build a world where compassion is not an aspiration but a reality.

Let The Journey Begin

The journey of compassionate leadership is both a personal and collective endeavor. It begins with self-compassion and extends outward, encompassing every level of the pyramid. As a reader leader, your role is vital in advancing these principles and creating environments where empathy and compassion thrive.

Where do we go from here? The answer lies in your hands. By embracing the transformative power of compassionate leadership, you can contribute to a future defined by kindness, justice, and shared prosperity. Together, let us travel from "i" to "We" to ensure that the legacy of the compassionate leader endures, inspiring generations to come.

This page intentionally left blank for your final reflection

_____

_____

_____

_____

_____

_____

_____

_____

_____

_____

_____

Chapter 15: Glossary

Actionable Compassion: The act of turning empathy into a tangible response, addressing the needs and suffering of others through deliberate and thoughtful action.

Adaptability: The ability of compassionate leaders to adjust and respond effectively to changing circumstances, challenges, and the unique needs of individuals or teams, ensuring decisions align with empathy and well-being.

Caring: A core characteristic of compassionate leadership involving genuine kindness and empathy, building trust and support within teams.

Collaboration: The act of working effectively with others, both within and beyond organizational boundaries, to achieve shared goals and societal betterment.

Compassion: A deep awareness of the suffering or needs of others, coupled with a desire to alleviate it through selfless action.

Compassionate Empathy: Intention + Action = A harmonious combination of empathy and compassion, where understanding others' emotions leads to purposeful and impactful actions to serve and uplift.

Compassionate Leadership: A holistic approach to leadership rooted in empathy, mindfulness, and altruism, focusing on the well-being of individuals and communities.

Compassionate Leadership Model and Pyramid: A unique leadership framework developed by Dr. Abraham Khoureis, emphasizing self-awareness, mindfulness, and progression from self-compassion to selfless service. This model inspires leaders to develop empathy, collaboration, compassion, and societal transformation.

Compassionate Leadership Pyramid: A seven-level framework within the Compassionate Leadership Model, guiding leaders from foundational self-compassion to the pinnacle of serving others selflessly. It emphasizes personal growth, empathy, and transformative impact on organizations and society.

Compassionate Society: A vision of a world where empathy, understanding, and mutual respect are foundational principles guiding policies, institutions, and interactions.

Community: A group of people sharing common interests, values, or geographical proximity, cultivating belonging and collective responsibility through empathy and collaboration.

Community Engagement: Active participation in local initiatives, events, and problem-solving efforts to strengthen relationships and encourage unity.

Concern for Well-being: Prioritizing the mental, emotional, and physical health of others, actively supporting their growth and success.

Culture of Compassion: An organizational or community environment where individuals prioritize acts of generosity, empathy, and mutual support.

Empathetic Compassion: The integration of intention (empathy) and action (compassion) to understand, connect with, and support others effectively.

Empowering Others: The practice of creating environments where individuals can thrive, grow, and achieve their potential through support and encouragement.

Family Tribe: The immediate circle of family members and loved ones who form the base of a leader's impact and serve as a support system for personal growth.

Flexible leadership: An adaptable approach where leaders adjust their style and strategies based on situational needs, balancing task-oriented and people-focused methods. It emphasizes responsiveness and pragmatism to effectively address diverse challenges.

Flexibility: The capacity to embrace change and adapt strategies while maintaining compassion and empathy.

Grassroots Change: Efforts initiated within local communities to address challenges and drive progress through collective action and compassion.

Intentional Empathy: The intentional ability to understand and share the feelings of another, marked by an internal desire to connect and relate to others emotionally.

Legacy of Compassion: The enduring impact of compassionate leadership, inspiring future generations to prioritize empathy, justice, and shared prosperity.

Local Environment: The immediate geographical and relational space where individuals interact with businesses, schools, healthcare systems, and other community structures.

Mindfulness: Being fully present and aware of one's thoughts, emotions, environments, and actions, ensuring alignment with values and promoting empathetic responses.

Missed Opportunity to Serve Others: Intention – Action = A scenario where empathy exists without follow-through, resulting in a failure to act on the opportunity to positively affect others.

Mutual Support Network: A system of reciprocal care and empathy among community members, businesses, and organizations to strengthen the local environment.

Next of Kin: A term encompassing close family, significant others, and chosen tribe members, who are foundational to developing compassionate leadership.

Noble Leader: A leader at the pinnacle of the Compassionate Leadership Pyramid who selflessly serves others, inspires societal transformation, and embodies integrity and profound empathy.

Open Communication: Encouraging honest and transparent dialogue, ensuring all voices are heard, building trust and collaboration.

Organization: A structured group of individuals working together to achieve common goals, guided by values of inclusivity, empathy, and social responsibility.

Own Tribe: A personalized support network of friends, family, and trusted individuals, providing emotional and practical support on the leadership journey.

Resiliency: The ability to endure and recover from challenges while maintaining a compassionate focus on others' well-being.

Ripple Effect: The cascading positive impact that arises from acts of compassion within one's family and tribe, extending outward to the broader community.

Self-Awareness: Engaging in introspection to understand personal strengths, weaknesses, and values, developing personal growth and alignment with leadership goals.

Self-Compassion: The foundational level of compassionate leadership, involving self-awareness, self-reflection, and intentional growth to enhance the ability to serve others.

Self-Reflection: The practice of thoughtfully considering one's actions, values, and decisions to improve leadership alignment and growth.

Serving Others: A principle where leaders prioritize the needs and aspirations of others, encouraging a culture of trust, collaboration, and compassion.

Serving Others Selflessly: The pinnacle of leadership where selfless service becomes the leader's focus, dedicating their actions to the well-being of others without expectation of personal gain.

Society: A broader community of individuals bound by shared values, laws, and institutions, working collectively for mutual well-being and equity.

Soft leadership: A people-centric approach that uses empathy, persuasion, and emotional connection to nurture relationships and influence others, prioritizing harmony and morale. It focuses on building trust and collaboration while encouraging a supportive environment for growth.

Systemic Equality: Addressing disparities in wealth, education, and access to opportunities to create a harmonious and equitable society.

Thoughtful Consideration: Deliberately ensuring actions and decisions minimize discomfort or harm, setting a standard for mutual respect and trust.

Understanding: A compassionate leader's ability to perceive and empathize with the emotions and behaviors of others, resolving conflicts constructively.

Unity in Diversity: The celebration and integration of diverse perspectives and experiences to create a cohesive and resilient community.

References

Armstrong, K. (2011). *Twelve Steps to a Compassionate Life*. Anchor Books.

Batson, C. D., & Powell, A. A. (2003). "Altruism and prosocial behavior." In T. Millon & M. J. Lerner (Eds.), *Handbook of psychology: Personality and social psychology* (Vol. 5, pp. 463–484). Wiley.

Dalai Lama & Cutler, H. C. (1998). *The Art of Happiness: A Handbook for Living*. Riverhead Books.

Davidson, R. J., & Begley, S. (2012). *The Emotional Life of Your Brain*. Penguin Books.

Davis, M. H. (1983). "Measuring individual differences in empathy: Evidence for a multidimensional approach." *Journal of Personality and Social Psychology, 44*(1), 113–126.

De Waal, F. B. M. (2008). "Putting the altruism back into altruism: The evolution of empathy." *Annual Review of Psychology, 59*, 279–300.

Germer, C. K., & Neff, K. D. (2013). "Self-compassion in clinical practice." *Journal of Clinical Psychology, 69*(8), 856–867.

Khoureis, A. (2019, September 20). *How to lead with compassion: A short guide for today's leaders.* Forbes. https://www.forbes.com/councils/forbescoachescou ncil/2019/09/20/how-to-leadwith-compassion-a-short-guide-for-todays-leaders/

Khoureis, A. (2020, January 16). *The making of the 'new capitalist': Shareholders, customers, and employees.* Forbes. https://www.forbes.com/councils/forbescoachescou ncil/2020/01/16/the-making-ofthe-new-capitalist-shareholders-customers-and-employees/

Khoureis, A. (2024). Making the case for compassionate leadership. *Leader to Leader Journal,* 2024(101), 25–30. https://doi.org/10.1002/ltl.20802

Khoureis, A. (2020, April 16). *In today's uncertain times, what leaders can do.* Forbes. https://www.forbes.com/councils/forbescoachescou ncil/2020/04/16/intodays-uncertain-times-what-leaders-can-do/

Khoureis, A. (2020, May 6). *When there is a clash of needs, leaders must practice empathy.* Forbes. https://www.forbes.com/councils/forbescoachescou ncil/2020/05/06/when-there-isa-clash-of-needs-leaders-must-practice-empathy/

Khoureis, A. (2020, May 27). *Seven mentorship secrets from an award-winning mentor.* Forbes. https://www.forbes.com/councils/forbescoachescou ncil/2020/05/27/sevenmentorship-secrets-from-an-award-winning-mentor/

Khoureis, A. (2021, January 19). *Reasonable accommodation: What leaders should know and do.* Forbes. https://www.forbes.com/councils/forbescoachescou ncil/2021/01/19/reasonableaccommodation-what-leaders-should-know-and-do/

Khoureis, A. (2021, November 17). *Key questions and systems for reinventing HR in the 21st century.* Forbes. https://www.forbes.com/councils/forbescoachescou ncil/2021/11/17/key-questionsand-systems-for-reinventing-hr-in-the-21st-century/

Khoureis, A. (2022, April 1). *The compassionate leadership pyramid: How to become a more caring leader.* Forbes. https://www.forbes.com/councils/forbescoachescou ncil/2022/04/01/thecompassionate-leadership-pyramid-how-to-become-a-more-caring-leader/

Khoureis, A. (2022, February 24). *What leaders need to know about decision-making.* Newsweek. https://www.newsweek.com/what-leaders-need-know-about-decision-making-1682033

Lutz, A., Brefczynski-Lewis, J., Johnstone, T., & Davidson, R. J. (2008). "Regulation of the neural circuitry of emotion by compassion meditation: Effects of meditative expertise." *PLoS One, 3*(3), e1897.

Neff, K. D. (2003). "Self-compassion: An alternative conceptualization of a healthy attitude toward oneself." *Self and Identity, 2*(2), 85–101.

Neff, K. D. (2003). "The development and validation of a scale to measure self-compassion." *Self and Identity, 2*(3), 223–250.

Preston, S. D., & De Waal, F. B. M. (2002). "Empathy: Its ultimate and proximate bases." *Behavioral and Brain Sciences, 25*(1), 1–20.

Ricard, M. (2015). *Altruism: The Power of Compassion to Change Yourself and the World.* Little, Brown and Company.

Singer, T., & Klimecki, O. M. (2014). "Empathy and compassion." *Current Biology, 24*(18), R875–R878

About Dr. Abraham Khoureis, Ph.D.

Dr. Abraham Khoureis, Ph.D., is a multi-talented thought leader and partner, author, and advocate for compassionate leadership. He is an adjunct professor who specializes in teaching graduate-level courses in business and management, blending academic theory with real-world business practices. Dr. Khoureis is also a small business owner and holds numerous state certifications and professional designations and licenses, showcasing his multidisciplinary expertise.

He is the creator of the Compassionate Leadership Model and Pyramid, which emphasizes leadership rooted in self-awareness, mindfulness, and a commitment to serving others without expectation of return. This seven-level model pyramid, with "Community" as its 5th level, reflects his vision of leadership that positively impacts the broader community and society.

Moreover, Dr. Khoureis developed the Disability Learning Attainment Model, a framework designed to empower individuals with disabilities through inclusive education, skill-building, and leadership development. His work champions and empowers inclusivity, accessibility, and ethical practices in both education and leadership. He has been published on *Forbes.com*, *Newsweek.com*, and the distinguished *Leader to Leader Journal*. He was recognized as LinkedIn's Top Leadership and Management Voice, and Thinkers 360's Top 50 Voices.

Dr. Abe's contributions extend to his writings, professional development initiatives, and thought leadership, making him a respected emerging leader in the fields of compassionate leadership, organizational behavior, and human development.

Easily accessible at: DrAbeKhoureis.com – DrAbeBooks.com
Social Media: @DrAbeKhoureis

159

Other Books by Dr. Abraham Khoureis, Ph.D.

The Balance In Between: Finding the Balance Between Emotional Intelligence and Emotional Stupidity
ISBN: 979-8-9895211-2-8

Hollywood Dream: How To Make It In Tinseltown
ISBN: 979-8-9895211-7-3

Decoding Microaggressions for Leaders and Beyond: Understanding Microaggressions Face-to-Face
ISBN: 979-8-9895211-4-2

Reasonable Accommodation: Empowering Inclusion
ISBN: 979-8-9895211-3-5

SELF: Discover the Many Types and Roles of Your 'SELF'
ISBN: 979-8-9895211-5-9

This page intentionally left blank for your final reflection

_____

_____

_____

_____

_____

_____

_____

_____

_____

_____

_____

www.ingramcontent.com/pod-product-compliance
Lightning Source LLC
Chambersburg PA
CBHW021232090426
42740CB00006B/493